VARIEGATED TAPESTRY
of
Ministry

PAPA MYLES-AIKINS

CREATION HOUSE

Variegated Tapestry of Ministry by Papa Myles-Aikins
Published by Creation House
A Charisma Media Company
600 Rinehart Road
Lake Mary, Florida 32746
www.charismamedia.com

This book or parts thereof may not be reproduced in any form, stored in a retrieval system, or transmitted in any form by any means—electronic, mechanical, photocopy, recording, or otherwise—without prior written permission of the publisher, except as provided by United States of America copyright law.

Scripture quotations are from the King James Version of the Bible.

Design Director: Bill Johnson
Cover design by Nathan Morgan

Copyright © 2011 by Papa Myles-Aikins
All rights reserved

Visit the author's website: www.pmylesaikins.com

Library of Congress Cataloging-in-Publication Data: 2011944547
International Standard Book Number: 978-1-61638-183-7

While the author has made every effort to provide accurate telephone numbers and Internet addresses at the time of publication, neither the publisher nor the author assumes any responsibility for errors or for changes that occur after publication.

First edition

11 12 13 14 15 — 9 8 7 6 5 4 3 2 1

Printed in Canada

Contents

1. The Nature and Necessity of Ministry 1
2. Theology and Ministry 5
3. Ministry as the Necessity of the Church 11
4. What Is Ministry? 17
5. The Requirements for Ministry 22
6. The Three Processes of Initiation into Ministry 36
7. The Relevance of the Adamic Ministry to the Contemporary Ministry 44
8. The Focus and Target of Ministry 52
9. The Apostle 62
10. The Prophet 67
11. The Evangelist 80
12. The Pastor 89
13. The Teacher 97
14. The "Body Gifts" 104
15. The Impact and Influence of Organization 114
16. Leadership 126
17. The Strategic Impact of Structural and Institutional Framework Within Leadership 137
18. Vision and Its Processes of Actualization 148
19. The Joshuaic Leadership Paradigm 156
20. The Danielic High-Profile Leadership Prerequisites (Dan. 1:4–8) 168
    Conclusion 176
    Glossary 177
    Index of Scriptures 179
    Index of Subjects 181
    Bibliography 183
    Other Books by the Author 185
    Notes 186
    About the Author 188
    Contact the Author 188

Chapter 1

THE NATURE AND NECESSITY OF MINISTRY

But Jesus answered them, My Father worketh hitherto, and I work.
—MARK 16:20

EVERYTHING DEFINABLE HAS A nature, and everything with a price tag has an element of necessity. It is within the above contexts that the nature and necessity of ministry emerge.

DEFINITION OF MINISTRY

Ministry is so pervasive, so profound, so elastic, and so dynamic that its definition requires periodic appraisal and redefinition.

Clearly, any definition of the term *ministry* must allow for as broad a latitude as the data of Scripture demands. However, two broad definitions of ministry emerge which give us a fair idea of this ennobled practical domain within theology:

- Ministry is a revelation of theology about the execution of the "kingdom business." The kingdom business is the work of the kingdom of heaven on earth through the church (Eph. 4:7–12).

- Ministry is the work of God, by God, through humanity, both inside and outside the church, relative to humanity and even extendible to the whole of creation. Because the domain of ministry encompasses the whole of creation, it behooves ministers to evolve pragmatic measures to safeguard nature, and occasionally to deliver an ecologically friendly sermon in order to encourage the preservation and proper stewardship of creation at large, without which there can be no humanity to carry out ministry.

God Himself is the chief environmentalist, which is why creation, in its early state, never had environmental problems. This unproblematic state of nature reflected divinity's environmental friendliness. So if ministry seeks to practically champion the cause of God, then environmental concerns ought to be given a place in the "belly" of ministry to project a holistic picture of ministry's operation and sphere of influence, which encompasses all of creation.

The Nature of Ministry

The nature of ministry is dualistic. There is a physical face of ministry as well as a spiritual face. The nature of ministry gives us a glimpse of the nature of God, reflecting as it does both His spiritual and His natural attributes. Thus true ministry considers both the physical and spiritual attributes of God.

The Spiritual Nature of Ministry

God is a Spirit, and therefore everything representative of or associated with Him essentially is spiritual (John 4:24). As a Spirit being, God's acts are first effected in the spiritual before translating into the physical realm. To illustrate this point, we can recall three major biblical examples that represent the pinnacle of divine acts.

1. Creation

Creation by God essentially was a spiritual act that manifested in the real and tangible, in that God did not create the universe out of any preexisting material substance (Gen. 1:1).

2. Salvation

Salvation for humanity, which came about through the death of the second Person of the Trinity, is essentially a spiritual act. The spiritual essence of this act becomes clear when we consider that the overriding impact of salvation is the recreation of the dead human spirit of the sinner (Rom. 8:8–11).

Consequently, the impact of salvation is first and foremost felt by our human spirit, leading to its recreation:

> And if Christ be in you, the body is dead because of sin; but the Spirit is life because of righteousness.
>
> —Romans 8:10

3. The "Day of Pentecost" Episode

The Day of Pentecost episode, which unveiled the ministry of the Holy Spirit through the official inauguration of the church, essentially was a spiritual act, notwithstanding the cloven tongues as of fire that sat upon the physical bodies of the hundred and twenty people who were in the Upper Room (Acts 2:3).

The ministry of the Holy Spirit evident in the Day of Pentecost episode is still experienced by the church, but the tongues of fire do not accompany it due to the fact that the church has already being established.

The Dynamics of the Spiritual Nature of Ministry

Everything that is spiritual is governed or activated by dynamics akin to their nature, hence the emergence of the spiritual dynamics or principles—the spiritual nature of ministry.

Messianic Ministry

The Messianic ministry stands out as both the embodiment and the standard bearer of ministry. Jesus prayed before the commencement of His ministry and sustained His ministry through prayers (Luke 4:1-2; 22:32-41).

Founding Fathers

The Founding Fathers of Christianity prized prayer above all other ministries, as seen in this quote from Acts 6:4:

> But we will give ourselves continually to prayer, and to the ministry of the word.

The Physical Nature of Ministry

The physical nature of ministry is necessary, indeed imperative; if ministry has a spiritual face, then it must also have a physical face. It is a ministerial truism that the spiritual emblems of ministry must operate within physical entities.

The Manifestation of the Physical Nature of Ministry

The physical nature of ministry manifests primarily through the various structures in the work of the church. For example, the establishment and placements of the fivefold ministries with their substructures like helps and governments profoundly attest to this notion.

THE EVOLUTION OF MINISTRY

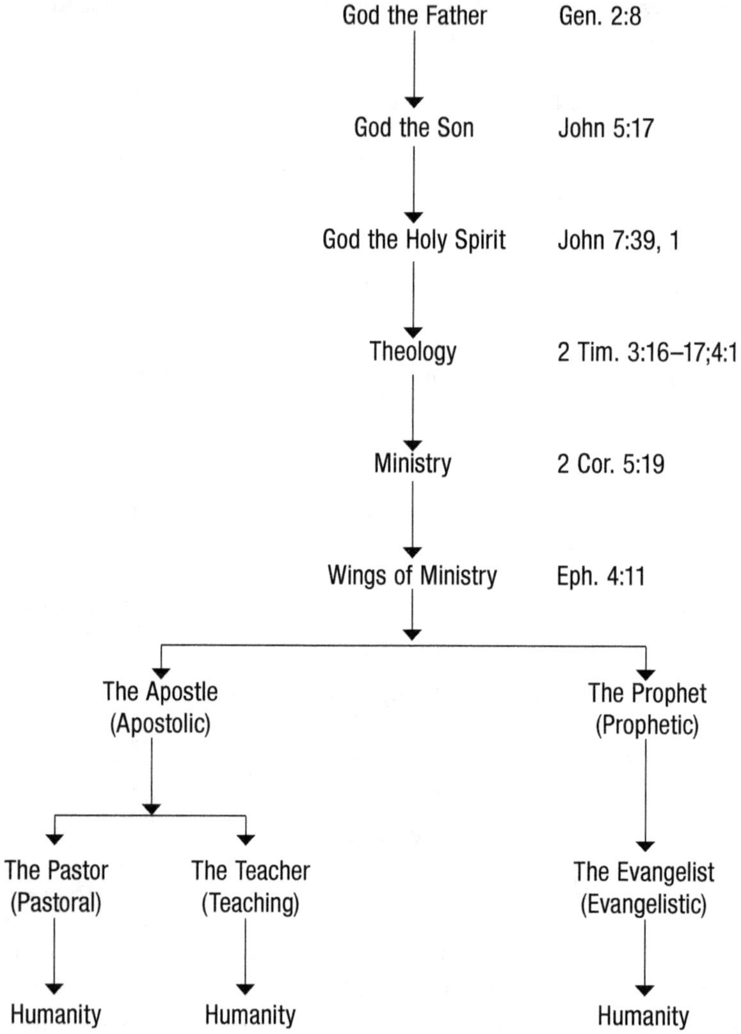

God the Father	Gen. 2:8
↓	
God the Son	John 5:17
↓	
God the Holy Spirit	John 7:39, 1
↓	
Theology	2 Tim. 3:16–17; 4:1
↓	
Ministry	2 Cor. 5:19
↓	
Wings of Ministry	Eph. 4:11

```
                    ┌─────────────────┴─────────────────┐
                    ↓                                   ↓
              The Apostle                         The Prophet
              (Apostolic)                         (Prophetic)
                    │                                   │
           ┌────────┴────────┐                          ↓
           ↓                 ↓                    The Evangelist
       The Pastor       The Teacher              (Evangelistic)
       (Pastoral)        (Teaching)                     │
           ↓                 ↓                          ↓
       Humanity          Humanity                   Humanity
```

Chapter 2

THEOLOGY AND MINISTRY

THE TERM *THEOLOGY* IS derived from two Greek words, *theos* and *logos*, the former meaning "God" and the latter "word, discourse, and doctrine."

The term *ministry* means the work of God, or God's work among humanity, through humanity. But in the broader perspective of divine ministry, ministry becomes God's work among humanity and His continued sustenance of creation.

This makes God as involved in humanity as He is in creation. Humanity is God's major concern, but creation also has a place in His heart, for without it there can be no man, and without man there would be no purpose for creation.

THEOLOGY AS THE SOURCE OF MINISTRY

For generations, theology has been considered the queen of the sciences, and today, ministry, by virtue of its attachment to theology, deserves to be labeled the maid of theology.

Just as a maid waits on her mistress for direction, guidance, and responsibility, so ministry waits on theology to make its mission of doing the work of God on Earth feasible. Without theology, ministry loses its cutting edge and becomes only a tinkling cymbal. It is theology that makes ministry sharp and relevant.

The concept of theology as the source of ministry can be seen in the typology of God as the source of man: theology is God and ministry is man. The analogy is that if man came out of God, then ministry undeniably comes out of theology.

THEOLOGY AS THE EMPLOYER OF MINISTRY

The relationship between theology and ministry goes beyond the analogy above, however, becoming akin to the relationship between an employer and an employee. Theology thus becomes the employer and ministry the employee, within the perspective that the employer is always bigger than the employee.

God (theology) created the Garden of Eden, and created a sort of employee, man (ministry), to keep it and dress it:

> And the LORD God planted a garden eastward in Eden; and there he put the man whom he had formed.
>
> —GENESIS 2:8

THEOLOGY AS THE COLLABORATOR OF MINISTRY

In creation the Trinity collaborated. When it came to the creation of man, the same principle of divine collaboration was in effect:

> And God said, Let us make man in our image, after our likeness.
>
> —GENESIS 1:26

Without collaboration, God ceases to be God within our human perspective. Through the collaboration between theology and ministry, humanity sees God, and by seeing Him can recognize Him as the creator of all and the God of all in addition to the other attributes ascribed to Him.

God created so that He could collaborate with man. He did not create to rule creation. Instead He empowered Adam to rule creation to underscore His collaborative mentality. Ministry exists as a facilitator of God empowered to rule over all human disciplines or at least benchmark it since generally, all human ways of collaboration seek to enhance humanity as a way of collaborating with God.

Every human being exists as God's collaborator, and it is in this truth that ministry assumes a universal reach. We can now give an accurate description of the functioning of ministry: God in man, with man, to man, and for God.

THE FIVE SENSES OF THEOLOGY

Theology releases—and its main means of release is ministry. Ministry sees—and its main means of seeing is theology. Ministry does not hoard what it sees but communicates it to humanity.

In addition to seeing, ministry hears, takes in through the mouth, walks, and touches with its hand. All these faculties are facilitated by theology, hence my coinage "the five senses of theology" or "the fivefold ministries." These five senses of theology are the means by which it expresses itself—through ministry.

MINISTRY AS THE EYE OF THEOLOGY

As one of the fivefold ministries, the prophetic ministry—which sees the evil in society and accordingly speaks against and rebukes it—operates on behalf of God. Thus this particular ministry shows that God is not distanced from and blinded to developments in the world but closely monitors them and voices His concern through His ministry agents on the ground among humanity. Jeremiah 6:10 gives us the gist of this, and Ezekiel 3:9 is relevant to the issue at hand:

> As an adamant harder than flint have I made thy forehead: fear them not, neither be dismayed at their looks, though they be a rebellious house.

Additionally, God uses prophetic eyes as a way of revealing hidden things to people. Thus God uses theology to make Himself known, and through the ministry of the prophets allows people to see what they could not see otherwise.

MINISTRY AS THE EAR OF THEOLOGY

What theology hears from God, it communicates to humanity through ministry. And theology is glad to intone, "After all, I have been a useful channel of rapport." On the strategic placement of hearing, Romans 10:14 is the quintessential verse:

> How then shall they call on him in whom they have not believed? and how shall they believe in him of whom they have not heard? and how shall they hear without a preacher?

MINISTRY AS THE MOUTH OF THEOLOGY

God speaks more than He acts. In the beginning, He spoke, and in the end, during His work in the Book of Revelation, He speaks. He was a speaking God, and He is a speaking God. Take the multitude of homilies that ooze from the podiums and ricochet the length and breadth of the world every Sunday, and your understanding will not be far from this truth.

When God speaks through theology and His words are manifested in ministry toward humanity, it debunks the deistic belief that though God created the world He does not "monkey" with it. Again, by speaking to humanity through theology and ministry, a personal God shows that He is in personal commerce with His creatures. Hebrews 1:1–2 can serve as the capstone to this point:

> God, who at sundry times and in divers manners spake in time past unto the fathers by the prophets, Hath in these last days spoken unto us by his Son, whom he hath appointed heir of all things, by whom also he made the worlds.

MINISTRY AS THE FEET OF THEOLOGY

God's omnipresence is evident in the role of ministry as the feet of theology. Ministry takes God along wherever it goes, and is therefore a vehicle for the Holy Spirit, who is present wherever ministry is taking place.

The Holy Spirit does not need ministry in order to be everywhere at the same time, but ministry reinforces His presence with the fruits of ministry as enshrined in Holy Ghost power, so that the beneficiaries and onlookers may truly say that "indeed God was here":

> And they went forth, and preached everywhere, the Lord working with them, and confirming the word with signs following.
>
> —Mark 16:20

Ministry as the Hand of Theology

The diverse spiritual gifts chronicled in 1 Corinthians 12—among them the gifts of faith, healing, and the working of miracles—represent the hand of God. The hand of God refers to God's divine nature manifested in unparalleled power, either by divine direct action or through human action to make it relative to ministry. It is through these actions that ministry is revealed as the hand of theology.

Ministry as the hand of theology avails itself of divine power to be channeled through it. For instance, God's revelation of Himself to Moses in the legendary burning bush episode described in Exodus 3:2 was theology in action:

> And the angel of the LORD appeared unto him in a flame of fire out of the midst of a bush: and he looked, and, behold, the bush burned with fire, and the bush was not consumed.

And Moses' commission to go and lead the Jews out of their bondage in Egypt after his encounter with the God who revealed Himself in the flaming fire marked the beginning of the Mosaic ministry. The pattern by which Moses became God's chosen instrument is a universal benchmark for ministry—calling, empowerment, and commissioning:

> Come now therefore, and I will send thee unto Pharaoh, that thou mayest bring forth my people the children of Israel out of Egypt.
>
> —Exodus 3:10

God's ultimate purpose in revealing Himself to Moses was to commission him to go back to Egypt from Midian to lead the Jews out of bondage in Egypt. The Mosaic pattern for entrance into ministry has repeated itself throughout history in the lives of God's chosen. Although receiving one's commission for ministry is the final step, without a prior distinctive calling and the requisite empowerment to fuel and drive the mission toward its destination, the whole process becomes a "holiday cruise and a funfair."

In summation, God's omnipotence manifests through His outstretched hand in ministry. The operation of the hand of God makes known His unlimited powers.

The Lord, who is called "Almighty" (Gen. 17:1; Rev. 4:8), is able to do all that He purposes.

TECHNOLOGY, THE FIRST HUMAN ENDEAVOR

Technology as the first human endeavor brings the dynamic attributes of God into play, and the introduction of technology to the Garden of Eden buttresses the point that theology is the father and mother of the arts and sciences, and the inspiration of all philosophies.

In God's commission to Adam to dress the Garden of Eden lay an explicit command to him to introduce technology as his first product. God provided the Garden of Eden, after which Adam had to use technology to produce the gadgets which would facilitate his work. And in so doing, Adam was fulfilling the primordial role of 1 Corinthians 3:9:

> For we are labourers together with God: ye are God's husbandry, ye are God's building.

THE EDENIC BENCHMARK FOR MINISTRY

The combination of two ministerial virtues—anointing and skill—is the Edenic benchmark for ministry. Anointing is the sole provision of God to the called to enhance and help actualize the vision that normally accompanies a divine calling. It can be seen from this analysis that, in Adam's case, the Garden of Eden was his anointing. The anointing is God's impartation to us to perform, and in Adam's case the Garden of Eden was to serve as his headquarters of empowerment. He was to sit there and rule, not to leave the garden and roam as he did.

However, anointing alone does not achieve optimum results in ministry. The anointing provided by God ought to be married to skills acquired through personal initiative by the called. This marriage ensures a synergistic ministerial performance.

Adam, as we have noted, was commanded to dress the Garden of Eden. To "dress" connotes altering the face of something in order to bring aesthetic beauty to it. Thus true ministry and the one in aesthetic beauty is the one factored around the anointing with the infusion of the acquired human skills.

In dressing the Garden of Eden, Adam subjected it to periodic evaluation and added value to it. Contemporary ministry therefore cannot skip this ministerial foundation; we must periodically "dress" our ministry by periodic appraisal for the following purposes:

- To infuse new ideas into the ministry

- To tap fresh anointing in the ministry to match the emerging new ideas
- To set new goals

Infusing new ideas into the ministry begets new goals for the ministry, and setting new goals for the ministry necessitates the tapping of fresh anointing to match the challenges that will emerge in the pursuit of the new goals.

Chapter 3

Ministry as the Necessity of the Church

GOD WAS THE REASON for theology; theology was the reason for ministry; ministry was the reason for the church; the church was the reason for man. Man was the reason for creation, and ultimately man was created for God.

God created in order to reveal Himself through nature to humanity. All that we see, know, have, and feel about God comes primarily from nature. Nature is the primary revelation of God.

In nature, God speaks powerfully and clearly that the vast world is established on a fixed and unfailing order, and that this order comes from a God who is Himself orderly and stable. David, caught in the maze of divine powers evidenced in creation, says it lyrically:

> When I consider thy heavens, the work of thy fingers, the moon and the stars, which thou hast ordained.
> —Psalm 8:3

The Evolution of the Church

Since creation, the church has gone through three evolutionary stages. The first stage of the church was the church of Adam; the second stage was the Old Testament church; and the third and perhaps the final stage is the New Testament church.

The Adamic Church or the Church of Adam

The Adamic church, or the church of Adam, was a solitary figure. It had Eve, Adam's wife, as an assistant. Adam as a church of one can be understood from the perspective that a church is a body in which dwelleth God. After his creation, Adam's being had two components: an earthly component and a spiritual component. His body was earthly, while his spirit was ethereal:

> And the LORD God formed man of the dust of the ground, and breathed into his nostrils the breath of life; and man became a living soul.
> —GENESIS 2:7

The composition of the Adamic church gives us a general picture of the nature of the church we know today: God-formed and God-animated. And from this perspective there seems to be a common element among the composition and function of all three churches in human history.

The function of the Adamic church

The structure and chain of command of the Adamic church made Adam the head, imbued with the spiritual properties of the fivefold ministries as manifested in the echelon of the New Testament church. Adam was expected by God to build the Edenic empire by training and bringing his assistant, Eve, to a level at which she could stand beside Adam and admirably complement his responsibilities:

> And the LORD God said, It is not good that the man should be alone; I will make him an help meet for him.
> —GENESIS 2:18

The same major spiritual factor that influenced the birth of Eve was the same factor that prompted the establishment of the sainthood to assist the fivefold ministries:

> And he gave some, apostles; and some, prophets, and some, evangelists; and some, pastors and teachers; For the perfecting of the saints, for the work of the ministry.
> —EPHESIANS 4:11–12

The parallelism of responsibilities between Adam and the fivefold ministries enjoins the fivefold ministries to live up to their responsibility by equipping the saints to be wise, knowledgeable, and responsible so that they may avert another catastrophe like the one in which Eve, the assistant of the church, became the tool that Satan used to destabilize the church.

Satan knows that he cannot directly attack God. But in trying indirectly to accomplish this feat, he attacks God's two master creations, man and the church. In attacking the church, Satan does not attack its spirituality but rather its human and its organizational elements. Once he holds sway over these, the organism of the church, in which the presence of God flows, becomes greatly retarded in its ability to function as it is intended to.

The fivefold ministries therefore must become an awakened watchdog with the body ministries of the church clustered around the sainthood.

A Graph of the Structure of the Adamic Church

The Habiru (Hebrew) Church

The word *Habiru*, for *Hebrew*, came from the Amarna tablets, which referred to the marauding Habiru, a people disrupting the normal political structure of Canaan. The Hebrews, or Israelites, represented the first corporate church of God.

Before the Exodus, God referred to them as His "sons," and during and after the Exodus, God dwelt among them in the form of His glory, first in a pillar of fire, and eventually in the tabernacle—as captured by the words of the writer of Exodus 40:35:

> And Moses was not able to enter into the tent of the congregation, because the cloud abode thereon, and the glory of the Lord filled the tabernacle.
> —Exodus 40:35

Common element

The common element between the Adamic church and the Hebrew church is evident in their formations. The Adamic church was formed from the dust of the ground, while the Hebrew church was formed in the fertile Nile Crescent region of Goshen. The only major difference between the two lay in the divine nature of Adam. Adam was imbued with divinity by the breath-of-life experience:

> And the Lord God formed man of the dust of the ground, and breathed into his nostrils the breath of life; and man became a living soul.
> —Genesis 2:7

Divinity dwelt within the Hebrew church as well, albeit corporately and not in the individuals who comprised the nation Israel. This movement from an individual divine nature to a corporate divine presence is attributable to sin, which had an effect on our first parents' relation to God, on their nature, on their bodies, and on their environment. Consequently, although God could not dwell within the individual sinner, He graciously dwelt among the Israelites as a corporate body after they had performed certain atoning rituals.

Media of revelation

God is omnipotent, omnipresent, and omniscient, and these attributes of His permeate His media of revelation. In the era of the Adamic church, it was the norm for God to walk with Adam in the Garden of Eden. There was no inhibition whatsoever in Him, especially with regards to His nature, which is absolute holiness, so long as Adam never acted contrary to the nature of God.

Before the Fall, Adam could go to God and God could go to Adam within the ambience of mutual understanding. But sin makes one a sinner, and sin separates one from God. God loves the sinner but hates sin. The sin nature of man necessitated the institution of the rituals to facilitate the dwelling of God's divine presence in corporate Israel.

A Graph of Divine Incorporation in the Hebrew Church

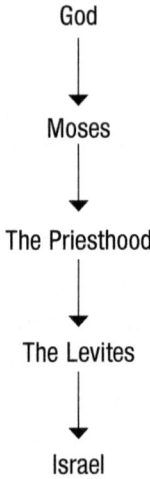

The New Testament Church

The New Testament church is symmetrical to both the Adamic and the Hebrew church from the perspective of its origin. The Adamic church was called from the ground after Adam's formation, in which the breath of life of God was given to make him a living soul. The Hebrew church was also called out from bondage in Egypt and given a lifeline when God's miracles and His presence made them His chosen ones among the then-heathen countries. And the New Testament church, which is technically named

Ecclesia, meaning "the called-out ones," is variously presented as the people of God (1 Cor. 1:2; 1 Pet. 2:4–10) and the company of redeemed believers made possible by the death of Christ (1 Pet. 1:18–19).

The vision of the church

The vision of the church serves as a window into ministry. And the church's vision can be known by the composition and functions of its anatomy and physiology.

The spiritual nature of the church

The church is dualistic in nature. It is both an organism and an organization. As the body of Christ on earth, the church reveals its spiritual nature by reflecting the various components of Jesus Christ—His being, nature, attributes, and values.

The reality of the church as a living organism is evidenced by the fivefold ministry gifts (Eph. 4:11). Once the fivefold ministry gifts are in their elements, and operate on full cylinders, the total church is well oiled and thoroughly lubricated to be impacted positively with the body gifts enshrined in 1 Corinthians 12:7–11 on full flight in the lives of the congregants:

> But the manifestation of the Spirit is given to every man to profit withal. For to one is given by the Spirit the word of wisdom; to another the word of knowledge by the same Spirit; To another faith by the same Spirit; to another the gifts of healing by the same Spirit; To another the working of miracles; to another prophecy; to another discerning of spirits; to another divers kinds of tongues; to another the interpretation of tongues. But all these worketh that one and the selfsame Spirit, dividing every man severally as he will.

The anatomical grouping of the body gifts

The body gifts of 1 Corinthians 12:7–10 can be divided into three anatomical groupings. These groupings—the hand of God, the eye of God, and the mouth of God—encompass the gifts mentioned above: word of wisdom, word of knowledge, discernment of spirits, prophecy, various kinds of tongues, interpretation of tongues, faith, healing, and miracles. These gifts represent the virtues of Christians as representatives of God; and when they are working in tandem in the body of Christ, the full power of the church is displayed.

The organizational aspect of the church is tasked with the duty of ensuring unity and synergy among the various offices and gifts which constitute the church as a living organism. Ultimately, the organization becomes the fulcrum of ministerial activity.

A Graph Depicting the Three Divisions of the Nine Gifts of 1 Cor. 12:7–10

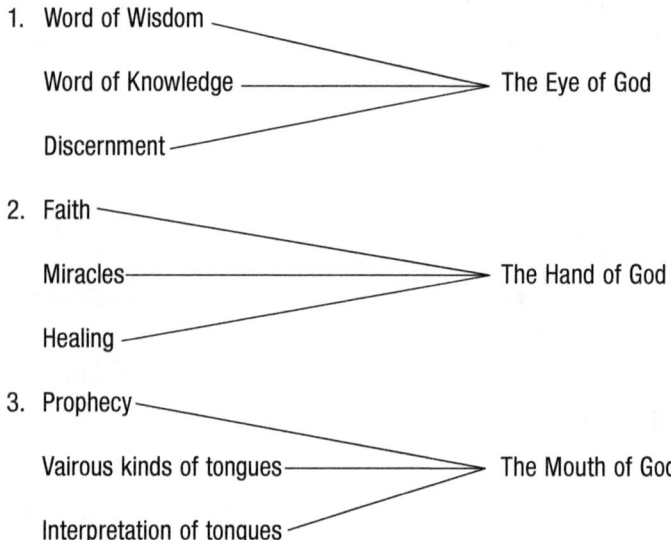

Chapter 4

WHAT IS MINISTRY?

CONSUMERISM, WITH ITS OVERWHELMING influence in the twenty-first century, and its insatiable appetite to devour or dislocate everything that comes its way, including the church, has the potential to cause a paradigm shift with regards to the tradition, vision, and purpose of the government (administration) and the governors (administrators) of the church. The church should be a window to look through for the definition of ministry, but today the ideals of ministry are fast eroding, leading to a gradual detaching of God from this once distinctive and sublime estate, which only strengthens the consumerism and other forces attacking it.

THE DEFINITION OF MINISTRY

The complexity of the anatomy and physiology of ministry makes it unseemly to give a solitary definition of the subject if it is to come under a holistic perspective and appraisal. Consequently, five definitions for ministry are given below, each of which describes a different facet. Taken together, these definitions afford a more complete understanding of the subject.

Ministry is the call of God for God

This definition of ministry is fit for those who have the calling of God on their lives and who are totally sold out to the One calling them.

Abraham heads the short list of notable Bible characters who fit this description. His call involved separating himself from his country, his kinsmen, and his father's house (Gen. 12:1) in order to become a stranger and pilgrim upon the earth. Abraham had the call of God, responded to God, lived totally for God, and was covenanted to God.

Moses comes next in line as a man who had the call of God upon his life. He received his call in the isolated Midian mountains:

> And when the LORD saw that he turned aside to see, God called unto him out of the midst of the bush, and said, Moses, Moses. And he said, Here am I.
> —EXODUS 3:4

Between Moses' life prior to the calling of God and Abraham's total separation from his country and kindred there is a common element. Both men's backgrounds were mandated by God.

And this treatise comes to full force with the addition of the Samuelic factor who, as a toddler, was given totally to God and had the nod of God as per this quintessential extract:

> And the child Samuel ministered unto the LORD before Eli. And the word of the LORD was precious in those days; there was no open vision....That the LORD called Samuel: and he answered, Here am I.
> —1 SAMUEL 3:1, 4

Christian workers within this bracket of ministry are very hard to come by. One is born into this world perhaps every three generations.

And when they appear, the monumental impact they leave behind, and the standards that guided them in their exploits, become unassailable several centuries after their demise.

We talk affably about people like Abraham, Moses, and Elijah, about their exploits and unique qualities, and yet, many centuries after their deaths, generation after generation has failed even to come near their achievements, much less equal the extraordinary exploits of those heroes of the faith. This knowledge, of which later generations of believers have fallen short, comes as a challenge especially to me, but it should impact the entire Christian workforce. If we are building on the foundations of the apostles and prophets, then we cannot lower the standards they have set.

Ministry is the empowerment of God for the manifestation of His power

God is all-powerful and able to do whatever He wills. This makes His power unlimited as it is seen and felt in all of creation.

Ministry power, the power needed to conduct ministry, forms but a fraction of the total divine power. Samson was an Old Testament figure used as an instrument to display God's power. His empowerment by God had less to do with ministry than with showing the power of God among the cluster of heathen peoples who surrounded Israel, notably the Philistines, who had by then become the Israelites' major oppressor. God instructed Samson's mother regarding his special upbringing and purpose:

> For, lo, thou shalt conceive, and bear a son; and no razor shall come on his head: for the child shall be a Nazarite unto God from the womb: and he shall begin to deliver Israel out of the hand of Philistines.
> —JUDGES 13:5

Calling, empowerment, commissioning

Ministry is initiated by three divine processes: calling, empowerment, and commissioning. When God calls a person, His integrity is staked on their future performance as a chosen vessel. He therefore makes Himself responsible for equipping and empowering the one called, so that they will be able to perform well.

Between the calling and commissioning stages comes the indispensable process of empowerment. Calling is important, and commissioning is indispensable, but it is empowerment that grounds them and propels them to the full realization of their potential.

When Jesus called and commissioned the early disciples, He demanded that they wait in Jerusalem for empowerment before beginning their ministry. God calls and commissions without human collaboration, but when it comes to empowerment, human cooperation is of paramount concern to God. When the Holy Spirit fell on the hundred and twenty disciples, they were in one accord with each other and with God, collaborating with His will by remaining obediently in the Upper Room as Jesus has instructed, waiting to be imbued with power from on high:

> And, behold, I send the promise of my Father upon you: but tarry ye in the city of Jerusalem, until ye be endued with power from on high.
> —LUKE 24:49

Nobody genuinely called and commissioned by God can enter the ministry without empowerment. Knowledge is an important requirement for ministry, and skill helps to ensure ministerial success, but empowerment is the major prerequisite for ministry.

The purpose of empowerment

The purpose of empowerment for ministry is twofold:

1. It propels the gifts and ministry potential in a person toward the full functioning of these virtues.
2. It defeats the powers of darkness that are perpetually at war with God, godliness, and the vessels of God. Isaiah 59:19 speaks to this effect of empowerment: "When the enemy shall come in like a flood, the Spirit of the Lord shall lift up a standard against him."

Ministry is responding to God's calling and working according to the purpose and intent of the calling

There are some people with conditioned or assigned calling. This calling appears to be the most delicate and intricate of all the types of calling. From those given a conditioned calling, God expects nothing less than inch-perfect and tailor-measured execution, and failure comes with dreadful ramifications.

King Saul is one of the major Old Testament characters who appears to have had such a calling. Saul decided to please God by hindsight, and displeased him by partial execution of his assigned responsibility to his calling, resulting in this rebuke in 1 Samuel 15:22:

> And Samuel said, Hath the LORD as great delight in burnt offerings and sacrifices, as in obeying the voice of the LORD? Behold, to obey is better than sacrifice, and to hearken than the fat of rams.

Discipline (or obedience) appears to be the major divine attribute expected of those with this calling. God acts as the "Father Minister," and all ministry points to God; therefore, as the God of discipline, He expects those who walk in His footsteps to tread cautiously and in consonance with this attribute.

Ministry is doing the work of God, with God, for God

This category of Christian worker appears to have some measure of all the flavors of the first three categories of minister. Their defining trait in ministry, however, is a strong consciousness that they are but inconsequential vessels in the hand of God, to whom glory and honor in ministry flows.

Paul, arguably the greatest Christian worker in the New Testament, falls in this category. Ministers of this rare species have a strong conviction of their calling, and of their separation unto God:

> Paul, a servant of Jesus Christ, called to be an apostle, separated unto the gospel of God.
>
> —ROMANS 1:1

Consider themselves dead but alive with Christ:

> I am crucified with Christ: nevertheless I live; yet not I, but Christ liveth in me: and the life which I now live in the flesh I live by the faith of the Son of God, who loved me, and gave himself for me.
>
> —GALATIANS 2:20

And give all to God; and God their ultimate desire:

> Yea doubtless, and I count all things but loss for the excellency of the knowledge of Christ Jesus my Lord: for whom I have suffered the loss of all things, and do count them but dung, that I may win Christ.
>
> —PHILIPPIANS 3:8

Such ministers do the work of God with a strong dose of God in their mind, willingly offering to Him the crowns and glory of ministry.

Today's ministry is self-focused. In such a milieu, where Christ hardly exists except as a faint shadow, the "Christ is heard, seen, touched, felt and experienced" message that Paul and company preached now exists only in old prayer books and homilies. And until the trend is reversed—until self gives way to Christ—the expectancy for the soon-to-break-out last revival in church history will remain a mirage.

Ministry is doing the work of God, period

Some are not called, yet they do the work of God. They do it for the love of God. Others are not anointed but do the work of God anyway, making up for their lack of anointing with Maccabean zeal. And still others are untrained, or inadequately trained, but notwithstanding, they push the Great Commission forward with infectious passion and fervor.

The work of God is the major occupation of these generalized workers, and they are not burdened by the theological requirements for ministry with which Christian workers in the first four categories are laden . To them, the power behind the "Go ye" commission is so strong that venturing out in fulfillment of Matthew 28:18–19 makes any earthly power seem infinitesimal by comparison with divine power:

> And Jesus came and spake unto them, saying, All power is given unto me in heaven and in earth. Go ye therefore, and teach all nations, baptizing them in the name of the Father, and of the Son, and of the Holy Ghost.

Ministry is a revelation of theology about how the church is conducted. If ministry is a revelation of theology, it must be true that ministry comes out of theology; and the phrase "how the church is conducted" connotes orchestration. This preamble reveals the nature and necessity of ministry; the addendum below addresses the scope thereof.

Theology takes center stage in ministry. Without theology there can be no ministry. Any ministry without a theological foundation is an institution of man and not of God. Man-made ministry is attempting blindly to do the work of God.

Man-made ministry usually results when people enter the ministry of their own volition, without the *a posteriori* call of God and its concomitant anointing upon their lives. True ministry is not an employment facility where candidates submit their resumés for employment.

True ministry is for the select few. God handpicked Aaron and his descendants for the priesthood, and later picked the Levites for His exclusive pleasure to help the priests in attending to the temple chores.

Chapter 5

The Requirements for Ministry

SPIRITUAL THINGS PERVADE PHYSICAL things. And fittingly, therefore, spiritual offices in the fivefold ministries are the highest offices on earth.

Presidential offices on earth are handed over to individual men and women by the people through electoral processes. But the spiritual offices as enumerated in the fivefold ministries are gifts from the Son of God through the Spirit of God to men and women for the work of God on earth: "And he gave some, apostles; and some, prophets; and some, evangelists; and some, pastors and teachers" (Eph. 4:11).

The enormous responsibilities that go with the lofty offices of the fivefold ministries impose entry requirements of the highest order on the officials who assume them, in consonance with the adage, to whom much is given, much is required.

Four broad criteria emerge as ministry requirements, and these are addressed below.

Responsiveness

Responsiveness is the first requirement of ministry. Responsiveness here entails a dual reaction. The first reaction is an affirmative response to God's calling; and the second is an affirmative response to the clarion call to the unknown and unseen face of the person out there who needs refreshment and consolation from your ministry. Responsiveness in this context therefore designates responsiveness to God for services unto humanity.

It will be theologically apt here to recall Moses' response to God's calling:

> And when the LORD saw that he turned aside to see, God called unto him out of the midst of the bush, and said, Moses, Moses. And he said, Here am I.
> —Exodus 3:4

God called Moses' name twice, and in doing so a major ministerial and relational principle was unveiled. First, any time God calls a person twice it signifies affection and acceptance of that person by divinity. Second, it assures the caller of the source of the calling to assuage skepticism. Third, it shows the acuteness of the call, and the urgency and swiftness with which the caller intends to address issues related to the call.

And in terms of the relational aspect, a double mentioning of a name or the repetition of a dream engenders certainty in the one being called.

Availability

Availability following responsiveness makes the chemistry right for God to begin His process of purification of the called. God calls Moses, Moses responds, and God demands availability: "Come now [be available now] therefore, and I will send thee unto Pharaoh, that thou mayest bring forth my people the children of Israel out of Egypt" (Exod. 3:10).

And out of this example unfolds an eternal ministry truth: when one responds to God without making oneself available to Him immediately, it renders the whole response half-baked.

Many in ministry have heard the call of God, but their lack of availability, which is crucial in the process of initiation into ministry, rendered their calling irrelevant to their intended purpose in ministry. As the saying goes, you can lead a horse to water, but you cannot force it to drink. And once the thirsty horse refuses to drink, no amount of force and intimidation can change its mind.

The calling of God is across the board; it is for every Christian, especially regarding the fivefold ministries. What separates the men from the boys, even in the same department of ministry, is availability. It is the measure of one's availability and responsiveness to God that determines the measure of the person in ministry.

Responsiveness is like one strike of the clock. It happens just once, but availability to God in ministry is a twenty-four-hour demand. The "holy law" of calling is that you respond only once to ministry, but the demand to be available in ministry is endless.

Elisha comes to mind here. Perhaps he was such an available minister that even in the grave the availability of his bones was enough to raise the dead. And Moses was so taxed with the things of God that Zipporah, his wife, and his two sons, Gershom and Eliezer, had to stay for long periods outside the camp of Israel with Jethro, Moses' father-in-law. Ministry demands twenty-four-hour availability to God in order to be able to replicate the works of Jesus Christ or of these great men from the Old Testament.

People often quote John 14:12 anticipatively—"Verily, verily, I say unto you, He that believeth on me, the works that I do shall he do also; and greater works than these shall he do; because I go unto my Father"—without associating this promise with the principle of availability to God, the fuel that drives the promise to realization. When you are completely available to God, God becomes completely available to you; and when God becomes completely available to you, every virtue in Him to enable you to fulfill John 14:12 becomes available to you in ministry.

Complete availability to God means availability of the heart, the mind, the eye, the ear, the emotions, the hand, and every other part of your being.

The divine economy operates around the interrelationship of commandments, promises, and principles. Consequently, taking a biblical promise in isolation from its associated principle would never yield the desired fruit, notwithstanding the Joshuaic faith you might put behind it. (Joshuaic faith here refers to the faith that could cause the sun to stand still for twenty-four hours.)

Similarly, you cannot live in wanton disregard for the commandments and expect the promises to come alive for you. That might even be suicidal. People for whom the biblical promises do come alive are dogged in obedience to the commandments, and these are people who walk under total divine favor. When one gets into the ambience of total divine favor, one is almost at the pinnacle of ministry, and, when one has reached this point, even natural laws could go tumbling at one's behest.

Empowerment—Spiritual

God's three major attributes—omnipotence, omniscience, and omnipresence—are theologically tagged as non-mortal. The implication is that divinity does not share these virtues with humanity. This theological assertion stems from the unfathomable nature of these attributes.

Omnipotence means ultimate power, or all-powerful; omniscience means all-knowing; and omnipresence means being present everywhere at the same time. The theologians were perfectly right in the exclusive ascription of these attributes to the divine. But there is a speck of correlation between the gifts of the Spirit as enumerated in 1 Corinthians 12:1–11 and these exclusive divine attributes.

Thus God, by His inestimable love and affection for humanity, has made us undeserved beneficiaries of His exclusive attributes, though marginally.

The gifts of the Spirit

Ministry is spiritual work, and spiritual work first and foremost demands spiritual tools. The gifts of the Spirit thus take center stage here. The fivefold ministry gifts (Eph. 4:8–12) are the primary gifts for the ministry, while the body gifts of 1 Corinthians 12:1–11 are secondary. But in this section, the secondary gifts come under microscopic evaluation.

The term "spiritual gifts" has two connotations, based on its etymological origin in ancient Greek. 1) Spiritual gifts (*pneumatika*, derived from *pneuma*, "breath" or "spirit") are supernatural manifestations which come as gifts from the Holy Spirit to operate through the believers for the common good of the church and even for the benefit of the unsaved. 2) Grace gifts (*charismata*, derived from *charis*, grace) are those spiritual gifts that involve both an inward motivation and the power to drive them.

These gifts are: word of wisdom, word of knowledge, discernment, faith, healing, miracles, prophecy, various kinds of tongues, and interpretation of tongues. These nine gifts come under three compartments or divisions:

1. The eyes of God
2. The mouth of God
3. The hand of God

The eyes of God

Those believers in possession of the spiritual gifts in the eyes of God division have the role of watchmen in the body of Christ, the church. The eyes of God gifts ensure that no enemy intrudes on, or charlatan deceives or operates in, the church.

The eyes of God gifts were wide awake and eminently in charge when Ananias did the unthinkable by pocketing a chunk of the proceeds from the sale of his land and lying to Peter, a deception which culminated in his death: "And Ananias hearing these words fell down, and gave up the ghost: and great fear came on all them that heard these things" (Acts 5:5).

Long before, the keenly covetous Gehazi, a servant of Elisha, had suffered a similar fate for lying, albeit in a milder form, as 2 Kings 5:25 relates: "But he went in, and stood before his master. And Elisha said unto him, Whence comest thou, Gehazi? And he said, Thy servant went no whither." Then, facing the wrath of the discerning Elisha, Gehazi had this for his "remuneration," as recorded in verse 27: "The leprosy therefore of Naaman shall cleave unto thee, and unto thy seed for ever. And he went out from his presence a leper as white as snow."

As I said, believers with the gifts of word of wisdom, word of knowledge, and the discerning of spirits are the watchmen of the church.

They sit on the walls of the church, as it were, in order to have a better view of an advancing enemy and of any act or deed antithetical to the sanctity of the body of Christ. And they do not exist only to view and report; they are armed to the teeth by the anointing of the Spirit on them to destroy the enemy as well as negative acts within the church. They are the troubleshooters of the church.

The mouth of God

Hebrews 1:1–2 serves as the preamble to a consideration of the mouth of God gifts:

> God, who at sundry times and in divers manners spake in time past unto the fathers by the prophets, Hath in these last days spoken unto us by his Son, whom he hath appointed heir of all things.

Prophecy, various kinds of tongues, and the interpretation of tongues are associated with the mouth of God with regards to the gifts of the Spirit (1 Cor. 12:10).

Prophecy

Prophecy as a "body gift"—the prophecy mentioned in 1 Corinthians 12:10—is to be distinguished from prophecy as a ministry gift, which essentially belongs to the top echelon of the church's leadership. As a spiritual manifestation, prophecy is potentially available to every spirit-filled Christian (Acts 2:17–18). Prophecy in this sense is one of the primary gifts of the Spirit for believers, and it is for comfort, encouragement, and exhortation. Prophecy enables a believer to bring forth a word or revelation directly from God under the impulse of the Holy Spirit.

Various kinds of tongues

During the inauguration of the church in Acts 2, speaking in various kinds of tongues was the primary discernible charismatic gift of those that fell on the believers: "And they were all filled with the Holy Ghost, and began to speak with other tongues, as the spirit gave them utterance" (Acts 2:4). It thus becomes imperative here to distinguish between speaking in tongues and speaking in various kinds of tongues.

Speaking in tongues is the generalized manifestation of the Spirit accompanying baptism in the Holy Spirit. Speaking in various kinds of tongues is a special gift used by the Holy Spirit for communicating between people of different languages should the need arise, as was the case in its maiden usage in Acts 2:7–8:

> And they were all amazed and marveled, saying one to another, Behold, are not all these which speak Galilaeans? And how hear we every man in our tongue, wherein we were born?

This distinction debunks the untheological argument that whoever speaks in tongues must speak in a particular discernible language.

Interpretation of tongues

Interpretation of tongues is a valuable gift: it enables the church to know the mysteries of God which are expressed through prophetic tongues.

When the Holy Spirit speaks to the church through a prophetic tongue, the interpretation of tongues gifts in operation in the church make it possible for the believers to know and understand what the Holy Spirit is saying. The gift may belong to the one who is speaking in tongues or to someone else who can interpret for them (1 Cor. 14:13).

The interpretation of tongues gift is a delicate gift, requiring total surrender of one's faculties to the Holy Spirit in moments of ministration. Without this surrender, one's own human thoughts could infiltrate one's mind and disrupt the interpretation of tongues. If not well controlled, the mind could "go shopping" in a moment for human rather than divine content, allowing this content to pollute the message being delivered.

Empowerment—the anointing

The anointing of the Holy Spirit is totally separate from the gifts of the Holy Spirit. The anointing is one thing and the gift another thing. The relation of the anointing to the gifts of the Spirit is that the latter complements the former.

A better understanding of the dichotomy between the anointing and the gifts can be gained from examining the four types and practices of anointing in the Hebrew tradition, which is foundational to the church tradition.

The practice of anointing with perfumed oil was a common practice among the Hebrews. The act of anointing was significant to the consecration for a holy or sacred use, hence the anointing of the high priest as recorded in Exodus 29:29 and Leviticus 4:3; and of the sacred vessels as recorded in Exodus 30:26.

Anointing was also an act of hospitality (Luke 7:38, 46). It was the custom of the Jews to anoint themselves with oil as a means of refreshing or invigorating their bodies (Deut. 28:40; Ruth 3:3; 2 Sam. 14:2).

Oil was used also for medicinal purposes. It was applied to wounds (Isa. 1:6), and used in connection with prayer for the sick (Mark 6:13; James 5:14).

The bodies of the dead were sometimes anointed for burial (Mark 14:8; Luke 23:56).

Of the four practices of anointing enumerated, the one relevant to the issue being addressed is the consecratory anointing. Primarily, the anointing of the Holy Spirit is given for services, and the consecratory anointing resembles it in this respect.

Types of anointing

Fundamentally there are two forms of anointing: the ceremonial anointing and the spirit-imparted anointing.

The ceremonial anointing

The ceremonial anointing dates back to the early days of the Israelite priesthood in the line of Aaron, which incorporates the Levitical initiation. The ceremonial anointing involves a process whereby oil is poured on a chosen person for initiation into ministry.

Its first instance took place when God told Moses to perform that rite for Aaron and his sons, as recorded in Exodus 28:41:

> And thou shalt put them upon Aaron thy brother, and his sons with him; and shalt anoint them, and consecrate them, and sanctify them, that they may minister unto me in the priest's office.

And still today the anointing is the maiden ritual for ordaining or consecrating people into the ministry of the Lord, at least within the evangelical fraternity.

Though a ceremonial overture, the presence of the Holy Spirit had come upon people who had gone through the ceremonial anointing during ordination or commissioning into ministry, or service to God:

> Then Samuel took the horn of oil, and anointed him in the midst of his brethren: and the Spirit of the LORD came upon David from that day forward. So Samuel rose up, and went to Ramah.
>
> —1 SAMUEL 16:13

The fundamental truth however is that not everybody's anointing invokes the Spirit of God to come upon the anointed.

It takes only the anointing on the divinely anointed to invoke the Spirit of God to come upon a newly anointed person.

Samuel went to Bethlehem from Ramah as God's anointed, and his anointing invoked the Spirit as he anointed David before David came under the power of the Holy Spirit. Just as vision affects and infects, so does the anointing.

If you truly walk with an anointed person you will certainly step into the shoes of that anointed person.

Joshua walked with Moses and became the next of king after Moses. Elisha walked with Elijah, and Elijah's mantle fell on him when his master was whisked to heaven in the second rehearsal of the rapture in Bible history.

The pioneer disciples walked hand in hand with Jesus Christ, and when our Lord was taken to heaven by the Holy Spirit, the Spirit returned to empower them for ministry to God in continuation of the tradition that when the anointed one departs, his mantle must fall on those that walked closer to him.

The Spirit-imparted anointing

The Spirit-imparted anointing is the anointing that falls expressly on the recipient from the Holy Spirit without the mode of the anointing oil.

This form of anointing differs from the ceremonial anointing from the perspective that it follows the sequence of fulfillment of certain conditions before its experience, and later a detailed treatment of the facilitating conditions.

Empowerment—mental

The mind or soul is the second person in the three-part entity of humanity. It has vast influence on both the spirit and the body, and in most cases the decisions of the mind carry along the inclinations or directions of both the spirit and body.

And if we go by the medical maxim that the sick person can only be pronounced dead if the mind is ascertained to have ceased functioning, then the mind truly is strategic to the fortunes of the whole being.

Consequently, God would not empower the spirit for services without room for divine mental connectivity via omniscience. The mental empowerment for ministry covers the wisdom and knowledge terrains.

Wisdom

Wisdom is defined by one school of thought as knowledge guided by understanding. However, the word *wisdom* carries with it such profound depth that a solitary sentence may not carry a comprehensive definition of it.

Wisdom is the fulcrum of life, both spiritual and physical. Every being, estate, and unfolding without it seems to be living in transition. Solomon therefore was apt on the topic in Proverbs 4:7:

> Wisdom is the principal thing; therefore get wisdom: and with all thy getting get understanding.

In ministry, wisdom is the primary key to success, with all other gifts settling for the secondary. The man touted as the wisest person that ever lived inherited the kingdom from his father totally disadvantaged.

He was young; he was naive; he was not a warrior; he was not as strong as David his father, and he had a feuding brotherhood to contend with. But he sought the right key in leadership, and because he found it, he was reputed to be the most powerful human that had ever lived, by the yardstick of fame, power, wealth, and influence.

One could have all the gifts and all the anointing in ministry, and yet lose them all if wisdom is not there for guidance. But one with wisdom can access the gifts and the anointing and hold them together in ministry until his or her demise from the world.

Things given to us by God can only be kept together through wisdom.

Knowledge

Knowledge is variously defined, but this is one of the best definitions: "deep and extensive learning."

This definition, no matter how profound it may be, is credited to a secular source. But godly knowledge, or the knowledge of God, which is the ultimate knowledge, is when humanity is gracefully illumined to catch a glimpse of the nature of God.

True ministry begins with relationships with God. This parameter is always mandatory before services to God and with God can be feasible—and from there service to humanity.

For instance, one cannot be in service to God without relationship with God, which shall provide insight into the type of services God would like him or her to render to Him.

Today many people are in ministry to self but not to God. They minister and do things in ministry, which do not have the endorsement of God. The reason? They fail to establish a relationship with God that would allow them to know the choice and taste God has for them in ministry.

If Saul knew the choice of God and yet could not perform to His expectation, ending up a casualty, what about those in ministry without a proper prior relationship with Him, and yet they think they are doing what He wanted them to do?

> And Samuel said, Hath the LORD as great delight in burnt offerings and sacrifices, as in obeying the voice of the LORD? Behold, to obey is better than sacrifice, and to hearken than the fat of rams.
> —1 SAMUEL 15:22

The complete minister is the one with reasonable knowledge of God through the Bible and theology, who is backed by a synergistic blend of all the secular disciplines of knowledge.

Paul was a successful, if not the most successful, minister for this reason: he knew God intimately, and he knew God via the most profound form of knowledge—revelation. Before then he had a wealth of secular knowledge.

But what tilted the scale in his favor in ministry was the revelation he caught of Jesus Christ, our Savior. He cries in sublimation of this experience clouded in serendipity:

> Whereupon, O king Agrippa, I was not disobedient unto the heavenly vision: But shewed first unto them of Damascus, and at Jerusalem, and throughout all the coasts of Judaea, and then to the Gentiles, that they should repent and turn to God, and do works meet for repentance.
> —ACTS 26:19–20

The anointing is the prime "virtue" in ministry, but without enough backup knowledge the Holy Spirit it is stifled in ministration. This is especially so in the exposition of the Word.

You first must have the Word, in Word exposition, before the Holy Spirit's anointing can articulate and activate the delivery.

Empowerment—physical

God does not provide a means to empower the spirit, the soul, and leave the body bereft of a similar deal to add weight to his overall purpose for the vessel He uses.

Fitness

Paul's intimation of body exercise profiting a little alludes to the physical empowerment of the body through fitness (1 Tim. 4:8).

During the life and ministry of Jesus Christ, He walked more than He traveled by boat. That was the era that humanity stayed closer to nature than to artificialities.

God's treasure for health and fitness can be conspicuously seen in creation prime to the embryonic stage of human life.

He rested on the seventh day as a way to teach us a profound biblical principle of health enshrined in fitness:

> And on the seventh day God ended his work which he had made; and he rested on the seventh day from all his work which he had made.
>
> —GENESIS 2:2

Eating

God's primary desire for the well being of our outer body is health, not healing. A healthy person does not need healing. And that is God's primary desire. Health maintains, healing repairs.

Consequently, God's preference for preventive health to therapeutic health could be seen in the detailed guidance to the Levites, and generally the Jews concerning sacrifices and rituals with regards to atonement.

He asked them to go for the meat while the fat was wholeheartedly requested for the altar to be burnt as part of the sacrifices to God as partly recorded in Leviticus 4:8–10:

> And he shall take off from it all the fat of the bullock for the sin offering; the fat that covereth the inwards, and all the fat that is upon the inwards, And the two kidneys, and the fat that is upon them, which is by the flanks, and the caul above the liver, with the kidneys, it shall he take away, As it was taken off from the bullock of the sacrifice of peace offerings: and the priest shall burn them upon the altar of the burnt offering.

Third John 2 is the New Testament rendition of and affirmation to this instant:

> Beloved, I wish above all things that thou mayest prosper and be in health, even as thy soul prospereth.

Eating discipline is one thing a great number of ministers lack, especially the successful and affluent ones. Because of the availability of their bottomless purchasing power, giving them hordes of options in all spheres of taste, they carry along their "banqueting table" wherever they go. They appear bloated and out of sort with fitness and health. These ministers can hardly remember the last time they fasted.

Romans 12:1 admonishes Christians to present their bodies as living sacrifices wholly and acceptable to God, and when this is observed, they become conscious of what to eat and when to eat.

No matter the level of one's anointing, if you are bankrupt in eating etiquette you will die and leave the anointing behind; for non-observance of certain physical laws does not necessitate the filling in of a self-created physical deficiency by a spiritual component.

The stark reality is that unless there is an intervention of miracles that mostly come when we are out of reach of physical solutions, spiritual laws primarily govern the spiritual entities just as the physical laws govern the physical entities.

There is always a thin line between the operation of spiritual laws and the operation of physical laws. You do not put a ship on a tarmac and expect it to sail just as you cannot put an airplane on the sea and expect to it to taxi off. Each must operate on its own terrain.

Sanctification

Sanctification is one of the major spiritual exercises that impacts the body and physically positions it for ministry. Sanctification primarily impacts the body in the sense that it is an exercise undertaken with the body.

However in ministry, every development in one region of the three regions of the human entity affects the other two entities; as it were, the spirit and the soul ultimately enjoy some of the accrual benefits of sanctification to the body.

Sanctification (Gk. *hagiasmos*) as used in the scriptures means "to make holy, to consecrate, to separate from the world, and be set apart from sin" in order that we may have close fellowship with God and serve Him.

Jealousy is one of the attributes of God. And as such He is a jealous God. However, God's jealousy is not definable by the human perspective of the Word, but by the divine perspective. And as such, God's jealousy is a holy jealousy that He manifests relative to people He has aligned Himself with.

When God aligns himself with a person, He does it in order to fully own that person. God does not own a person and allow the person to divide his allegiance to him with any being, not even oneself. This is sacrosanct.

People who play down this high-premium ministry requirement of sanctification experience to the full the calamitous ramifications of their acts. Samson is a notable character:

But the Philistines took him, and put out his eyes, and brought him down to Gaza, and bound him with fetters of brass; and he did grind in the prison house.

—Judges 16:21

Ministerial covenants

Samson had a covenant with God, or rather, God had a covenant with Samson. The covenant was the Nazarene covenant. In this covenant, Samson was expected to ensure that no razor touched his hair. He reneged on the covenantal promise, and the consequence is seen in the quoted scripture.

Any minister who has the calling of God upon his life consciously or unconsciously has a covenantal linkage with God. It thus becomes imperative for the "called" ministers to seek verifications from God what their ministerial covenants are.

Once a minister knows his covenantal obligations and rigorously sticks to it, his relationship with God becomes inviolable, and such people are able to access all the divine support for ministry right from the inception of their ministries to their calling back home after the fulfillment of their ministerial sojourning.

I do not have to labor the point that great men and women of God are men and women with sanctification very high on their spiritual agenda. Such ministers are deep in sanctification, high on sanctification, and broad by sanctification.

To such ministers sanctification is the cutting edge of their ministries, as it was for our Lord and Savior Jesus Christ, exemplified in impact here via Luke 8:28:

> When he saw Jesus [the legion] he cried out, and fell down before him, and with a loud voice said, What have I to do with thee, Jesus, thou Son of God most high? I beseech thee, torment me not.

Being studious, and knowing the Scriptures thoroughly as a minister, does not scare the devil much if you are bereft of the virtues of sanctification.

Satan knows God better, and for that matter the Word of God better, for he was with God until his rebellion; otherwise, how could he have taken on the Word of God Himself in the battle of words, with only one extraction of that confrontation here to suffice:

> Then the devil taketh him up into the holy city, and setteth him on a pinnacle of the temple, And saith unto him, If thou be the Son of God, cast thyself down: for it is written, He shall give his angels charge concerning

thee: and in their hands they shall bear thee up, lest at any time thou dash thy foot against a stone.

—Matthew 4:5–6

The process of sanctification

Sanctification is not a one-shot acquisition product or estate. It is an estate which is unending in acquisition.

You seek it daily; that means sanctification is a daily requirement. You do not get it one day and go to sleep with it forever. If you get it one day and think that is the end of it all you risk losing it altogether.

Sanctification is a journey; and sanctification is a way of life. As a journey, a minister must undertake it; and as a way of life, a minister must live by it, live in it, and live with it. Sanctification as one of the core requirements of God for ministry is unattainable in a lifetime.

Also sanctification is not something you desire. It is something that mere desire does not satisfy. Sanctification is something you must thirst and hunger for.

The nature of sanctification is that when you are satisfied after you desire it, you must desire it again the next day, and on and on, until the end of your ministry on earth.

And Paul, alluding to sanctification here, and mindful of its grave ramifications, says:

> But I keep under my body, and bring it into subjection: lest that by any means, when I have preached to others, I myself should be a castaway.
>
> —1 Corinthians 9:27

Keeping his body and bringing it into subjection was Paul's description of a daily practice of sanctification, and it couples as the universal benchmark for this sacred theme.

The hand of God

God's omnipotence is projected in the "body gifts" through the power gifts—faith, miracles, and healing.

Faith

Faith takes first place among the power gifts. As the catalyst to the operation of all the gifts of the Spirit, faith becomes even more pronounced in the facilitation of the other power gifts—miracles and healing.

Miracles

Miracles are acts that supernaturally restore a situation to the state God intends. For example, when a deaf person is able to hear again after prayer, that person could be said to have received a miracle.

Healing

Healing is the art of praying for the sick to recover from their ailments. In the early days of the church, healing became an integral part of the apostles' ministry. Healing also became very prominent during most of the revival eras in church history.

Chapter 6

THE THREE PROCESSES OF INITIATION INTO MINISTRY

MINISTRY IS DIVINELY ORDERED and designed, hence its detail in accordance with God as the God of order, design, and detail. And out of these attributes of God emerge the process of calling, empowerment, and initiation into ministry. God plans, programs, and prepares prior to the commencement of anything and everything. First, God calls people into His plan, and then He empowers them to take part in the programs envisaged in the plan, which climaxes with their initiation into doing the work of the plan.

When a person is initiated into ministry, people only see the fruits of the initiation—a man or woman ministering—without much information about the larger, behind-the-scenes work of calling and empowerment that preceded the initiation.

CALLING

A broad-spectrum analysis of divine calling reveals four levels of calling. These are:

1. Calling into Christendom
2. General calling into ministry
3. Acute calling
4. Conditional calling

CALLING INTO CHRISTENDOM

Hypothetically, Christianity is the only experiential religion. Though experiences are subject to different interpretations, both the pervasive impact of Christianity and its uniqueness from all other religions arise from the human/divine intrarelationship and interrelationship experienced by the believer.

THE HUMAN/DIVINE INTRARELATIONSHIP

When a person is "born again" to become a Christian, the result is that that person's hitherto dead human spirit is recreated, infused with new life by the spirit of the

Trinity—the Father God, the Son God, and the Spirit God—who come to dwell in the person's heart (Rom. 8:9–11). Thus 2 Corinthians 5:17 becomes a reality: "Therefore if any man be in Christ, he is a new creature: old things are passed away; behold, all things are become new."

Then, after the new birth, the indwelling trinitarian Spirit remains with the believer and begins a lifelong relationship with his recreated human spirit to make the human/divine intrarelationship feasible as well as practicable.

Inferentially, therefore, Christianity involves the calling of individuals by God into a human/divine intrarelationship. And no scripture expresses this better than 1 Peter 2:9:

> But ye are a chosen generation, a royal priesthood, an holy nation, a peculiar people; that ye should shew forth the praises of him who hath called you out of darkness into his marvellous light.

Christianity is the calling to life by God of our dead human spirit. Etymologically, *calling* is derived from the ancient Greek word *kaleo*, whose meaning puts indubitable weight behind this argument.

The Human/Divine Interrelationship

God is the greatest communicator. He communicates with us to enable us to communicate with Him.

Everything about nature bespeaks the communicative ingenuity of God. When we breath in, we experience God's message of life to humanity. When the rains come down, behind the outpouring is the assuring message of sustenance to humanity. When the sun emerges in the east in the morning, divinity is behind it with the whisper: "There is hope for you." And when a child is born, behind its birth throes is the inescapable perpetuity of life, symbol of the fruit of human love between male and female, a pale reflection of the holistic divine love which is inestimable and invisible.

But the greatest manifestations of the human/divine interrelationship are our recreated human spirit, and the impartation of the theophanic manifestation, accessible to us through the written Word (*logos* and *rhema*), the anointing of the Spirit, and the glory of the Father God.

By the charismatic gifts, God opens Himself up for us, makes Himself accessible so that we can also be accessible to Him as He seeks to fill us with everything in Him: "And there appeared unto them cloven tongues like as of fire, and it sat upon each of them. And they were filled with the Holy Ghost, and began to speak with other tongues, as the Spirit gave them utterance" (Acts 2:3–4).

This extract on the *kabod*, God's glory, from Walter Eichrodt's *Theology of the Old Testament* takes us further into our understanding of the subject:

> The deadly effect of such a vision means that this petition cannot possibly be granted; it is by a special gift of God's favour that Moses is finally allowed to see the divine glory pass before his veiled eyes, at any rate from behind, that is to say at extreme edge and outskirts.[1]

General Calling

Primarily, Christianity is a mass calling with a level playing field. God's love is transcendent, and so is His gift.

God's love knows no frontiers, no barriers; rich and poor, men and women all enjoy this love equally. The boundlessness of God evident in His love is also discernible in the opportunities He offers humanity. As the God of justice, He does not put one individual ahead of another with regard to the opportunities He offers us to serve Him

In the time of the Old Testament, the Israelites (Jews) were especially chosen as the people through whom the divine machinery for redemption was channeled. However, during Christ's earthly ministry, God's attribute of justice was in full force, sidelining the Jews but giving the Gentiles the first taste of it:

> He came unto his own, and his own received him not. But as many as received him, to them gave he power to become the sons of God, even to them that believe on his name.
>
> —John 1:11–12

Though bypassed in this first round of empowerment after the coming of Christ, the time of the Jews grows nearer as we are about to close the chapter on the Gentile age spoken of in this Pauline revelation:

> For I would not, brethren, that ye should be ignorant of this mystery, lest ye should be wise in your own conceits; that blindness in part is happened to Israel, until the fulness of the Gentiles be come in.
>
> —Romans 11:25

Privileges necessitate responsibilities, and God's general calling reflects this philosophy. The "Go ye therefore to all nations" command is associated with the mass calling of God. In Christianity no one sits on the fence; to wit, there is no armchair Christianity.

Just as God created Adam and put the Garden of Eden under his care to keep it, so He has committed to us the evangelization of the world: "Go ye therefore, and teach all nations, baptizing them in the name of the Father, and of the son, and the Holy Ghost" (Matt. 28:19). Our calling into the Great Commission is therefore a general calling intended for all Christians, not one reserved for a coterie of experts.

Salvation through belief in Christ is the greatest privilege accorded humanity, and its accompanying responsibility—"Go ye"—indisputably qualifies as the most enviable among all the sublime responsibilities that accompany our privileges as Christians.

Calling into the Fivefold Ministries

The calling into the fivefold ministries essentially is a New Testament calling.

Exegesis of Ephesians 4:7–11 reveals that the fivefold ministry gifts were so dear to Christ that He assessed the ministry needs of the church before He ascended on high and gave the gifts of the Holy Spirit to His followers, imparting them upon men and women fit to lead the church and perform great acts of service within it: "But unto every one of us is given grace according to the measure of the gift of Christ" (Eph. 4:7).

The fivefold ministries are: 1) apostle, 2) prophet, 3) evangelist, 4) pastor, 5) teacher. As a whole chapter ahead is devoted to a comprehensive treatment of these ministries, this primer on the subject will suffice for now.

Acute Calling

Moses' calling to lead the Jews out of slavery to the Promised Land in fulfillment of the covenant between God and Abraham fits well into the category of the acute calling. Samuel also qualifies to be counted as one with an acute calling on his life. Acute calling pertains to a particular crisis; it is a calling God bestows by putting somebody in a special spiritual position for a unique assignment.

The exceptional people who receive acute callings are scarce gems ennobled and enabled by a unique grace and power commensurate with the Herculean challenges associated with their calling.

Acute or crisis calling could also be called "fire calling." The phrase "fire calling" suggests believers with a call on their lives who are associated with fire. These were either called out of fire, or were nurtured around fire, with Exodus 3:3–4 serving as the first example:

> And Moses said, I will now turn aside, and see this great sight, why the bush is not burnt. And when the LORD saw that he turned aside to see, God called unto him out of the midst of the bush, and said, Moses, Moses. And he said, Here am I.

And then the continuation of this theme in 1 Samuel: "And ere the lamp of God went out in the temple of the LORD, where the ark of God was, and Samuel was laid down to sleep" (3:3).

In Moses' experience, the God of fire had to manifest Himself in a very dramatic way, with the manner of manifestation quite unconventional. This theophanic manifestation suggested a crisis period for God to pick a worthy and prepared leader to lead His chosen people, the Jews, out of Egypt in fulfillment of His covenantal promises to Abraham.

Samuel's experience completes the theme. Eli, the high priest, was about to fall asleep. His two sons, who were potential successors to the esteemed office of the high priest, had opted out by virtue of their despicably immoral behavior. At that point in time, God had a need for an apprentice high priest, and in order to fulfill that need, He had to create a need for someone else—Hannah, the eventual mother of Eli's successor.

To resolve the crises of both God and Hannah, a deal was struck. God answered Hannah's need for a biological son, and Hannah answered God's need for a covenantal son to replace Eli. She offered up Samuel, her son, into covenant with the Lord:

> And she vowed a vow, and said, O LORD of hosts, if thou wilt indeed look on the affliction of thine handmaid, and remember me, and not forget thine handmaid, but wilt give unto thine handmaid a man child, then I will give him unto the LORD all the days of his life, and there shall no razor come upon his head.
>
> —1 SAMUEL 1:11

Individuals acutely called are people with great testimonies linked to their birth. Moses was preserved in defiance of the pharaoh's fiat that all children born in his era must be strangulated at birth. And Samuel was born when all odds were stacked against his mother, with the prospect of perpetual barrenness confronting her.

CONDITIONAL CALLING

When God chose Saul for the kingship of Israel, his establishment on the throne was conditional, and at his disobedience the kingdom was taken away, though not immediately:

> And Samuel said to Saul, Thou hast done foolishly: thou hast not kept the commandment of the LORD thy God, which he commanded thee: for now would the LORD have established thy kingdom upon Israel for ever.
>
> —1 SAMUEL 13:13

And when Solomon ascended his father's throne, God tied the sanctity and continued existence of the Davidic throne to obedience. He made it clear that the kingdom would endure only if subsequent kings in the line of Solomon, arguably Israel's greatest king, obeyed Him. Second Chronicles 7:17–18 succinctly endorses this contention:

> And as for thee, if thou wilt walk before me, as David thy father walked, and do according to all that I have commanded thee, and shalt observe my statutes and my judgments; then will I stablish the throne of thy kingdom, according as I have covenanted with David thy father, saying, There shall not fail thee a man to be ruler in Israel.

The gifts of God are many and varied; and so are His callings. For this reason, we can put forth a theological and ministerial proposition that God treats us differently, whether as His children, or as those in any category of His calling.

That is why one does not have to be a copycat of one's mentor or role model. It is good to learn and take inspiration from people, but it is ministerial suicide to attempt to replicate the ministry of anyone. God made you to be you, and God made that person to be that person.

We are all different in personality; and the celebrated Rick Warren gives this truth vivifying force:

> You can learn from the examples of others, but you must filter the lessons you learn through your own shape.[2]

Saul disobeyed once, and that cost him the throne and eventually his life. David committed adultery with Bathsheba, and capped it by murdering her husband, Uriah, yet the major consequences of those acts were reserved for his offspring. That is the God of conditional calling, and that is why we must avoid making attempts at ministerial replication.

EMPOWERMENT

Moses' experience of calling, empowerment, and initiation is paradigmatic in ministry. Moses lived in Pharaoh's palace for forty years in order to undergo tutelage in diplomatic governance. After "graduating" with what we might call his "Ph.D. in diplomatic governance," he was banished into the Midian desert to begin another forty years of schooling at the "University of Divine Encounter," this time receiving preparation for his encounter with the theophanic manifestation depicted in Exodus 3:2:

And the angel of the LORD appeared unto him in a flame of fire out of the midst of a bush: and he looked, and, behold, the bush burned with fire, and the bush was not consumed.

In all, Moses went through seven steps in his process of empowerment.

THE SEVEN-STEP MOSAIC EMPOWERMENT PROCESS

1. Denunciation
2. Diversion
3. Leaning
4. Boldness
5. Hand of miracles
6. Turning from the five senses
7. Bodily transformation

In the course of my studies, I have discovered that there are "big callings," "medium callings," and "small callings" in God's scheme of calling. I have also realized that God does not use a single measurement for the preparation of the called. For every calling there is a commensurate level of preparation.

The bigger the calling, the bigger and more extensive the preparation. The diligence by which God prepares the called hinges on the fact that every calling of God is accompanied by a measure of anointing, which invariably brings the presence of God to bear on the called.

And because any mishap on the part of God's called ultimately casts a slur on Him, God for His part ensures the adequate and thorough preparation of the people He calls before pushing them out onto the "streets" to commence hostilities with the devil.

BRIEF EXEGESIS OF THE MOSAIC EMPOWERMENT PROCESS

1. *Denunciation* (Exod. 3:5): Remove shoes. The shoe represents royalty and pride.
2. *Diversion*: Removal of shoes means doing away with the symbol of one's pride, which significantly is the means by which you come in contact with the filth of this world.
3. *Leaning* (Exod. 4:3): The rod Moses used was what he leaned on during his challenging assignment of shepherding the Israelites.

4. *Boldness* (Exod. 4:4): Moses caught the tail of the serpent, symbolizing a tutorial in boldness.

5. *Hand of miracles*: The sign of the serpent symbolized the miracle Moses was to perform before his encounter with Pharaoh.

6. *Turning from the five senses*: Moses' bosom represented his five sensual feelings, which his hand had to go through as a turning away from the five senses to the sixth sense—faith.

7. *Bodily transformation*: The second hand-in-bosom experience symbolized total bodily transformation—empowerment for the rigorous ministry work.

Chapter 7

THE RELEVANCE OF THE ADAMIC MINISTRY TO THE CONTEMPORARY MINISTRY

ONE COULD ANALOGIZE THE evolution of ministry from the Adamic era to the present era with the forms of God's self-manifestation.

God's self-manifestation to humanity, broadly or technically termed *theophany*, was processional; and this feature is also markedly relevant in the evolution of ministry. God's self-manifestation to humanity has been appreciated on the peripheral, and the concomitant impact of this is the manifested lousiness in ministry.

And on this appreciation of God's self-manifestation Eichrodt has this to say:

> That God can without detriment to his majesty give visible evidence of his presence on earth is a conviction taken as much for granted by Israel as by other nations.[1]

Three major eras emerge in the evolution of ministry: ministry in the pre-Fall era, ministry in the Old Testament era, and ministry in the New Testament era.

MINISTRY IN THE PRE-FALL ERA

Adam was created for ministry—ministry to God and ministry to self. This was the Adamic ministry. Adam's ministry to God was to show appreciation to Him for giving him life, his wife, Eve, the Garden of Eden as his headquarters of governance, and creation at large.

THE ADAMIC MINISTRY

Unchangeability is one of the pervasive attributes of God. God never defaces, He never changes, and He never ages. From generation to generation, God is the evergreen God.

And in so far as God does not change in nature, He does not change in His acts, and deeds, and ways also. Thus His unchangeable nature is resplendent in His acts, deeds, and ways. Ministry is replete with these virtues of God. When God calls, He calls to commission. And when He commissions, it is preceded by empowerment. He does not call us and tax us insufficiently equipped.

Adam's inception, empowerment, and commissioning exuded these traits; and had been the sequence through the line of ministry:

> And God said, Let us make man in our image, after our likeness: and let them have dominion over the fish of the sea, and over the fowl of the air, and over the cattle, and over all the earth, and over every creeping thing that creepeth upon the earth.
>
> —Genesis 1:26

The Adamic ministry was tripartite in nature and scope with broad based individual segments. The primary, or first ministry of Adam and Eve was to be in charge; the secondary ministry was to dress, and the third ministry was to keep (Gen. 2:15).

Put Him (Be in Charge)

The Hebrew word for put: *suwm* (soom) has a great variety of applications. However these three picks: appoint; commit; and determine, come for evaluation due to the helpful roles they play relative to the treatise under scrutiny.

Appoint

God is a God of order and discipline. In this wise God's structure is always conspicuous in His dealing with humanity and in the functionality of the kingdom of heaven.

And even within the Trinity, God cannot help but bring this attribute into play, hence the designation—the Father God, the Son God, and the Spirit God.

Therefore, God, in putting Adam in the Garden of Eden, meant appointing him to the sublime office of the president of all created things visible and invisible. This means Adam had the power and vested authority to even rule and reign over all the angels, including Satan.

Employing biblical exegesis to aid our cause, Psalm 8:4–5 appears to be the best port of call:

> What is man, that thou art mindful of him? and the son of man, that thou visitest him? For thou hast made him a little lower than the angels, and hast crowned him with glory and honour.

The etymology of the word *angel* used in Psalm 8:5, and which is under exegesis here, is *malak*. *Malak,* properly used means "deputyship." In this instant, Adam appeared to be the first deputy of God, the highest in the hierarchical order of all created beings, visible and invisible.

Probing into theophany the theologically adept Eichrodt offers an insightful tuition relative to the *malak yhwh*:

> Among the narratives relating to the angel one particular group stands our because it describes an emissary of Yahweh who is no longer clearly distinguishable from his master, but in his appearing and speaking clothes himself with Yahweh's own appearance and speech.[2]

Commit

Commitment entails a person working within a certain earmarked domain. To this end was Adam appointed. He was appointed to be responsible.

When a person is entrusted with a certain responsibility, the mode of appraisal is their action or inaction relative to that responsibility. Therefore responsibility, or commitment, goes with every appointment.

That was why God punished both Adam and Eve when they faltered by their irresponsible act of obeying Satan and handing over the governorship of the earth into His hands. Remember, Satan implicitly alludes to this fact in his brief encounter with Jesus Christ (the second Adam) in Luke 4:6:

> And the devil said unto him, All this power will I give thee, and the glory of them: for that is delivered unto me; and to whomsoever I will I give it.

Responsibility is one of the salient and humanly discernible attributes of God. For instance, when God created the world, it could be likened to appointment in that He appointed the world to be there. He has then been responsible for its maintenance, at least within the purview of creation that there are certain features within creation responsible for the maintenance of creation.

Thus the principle of every appointment goes with a responsibility, with the concomitant honor or punishment; for fulfillment or failure, respectively, comes into play here. That is the God of principle for you, and that is how the God of principle expects His sons and daughters to conduct themselves, and minister, within the courts of the Almighty.

And know that only responsible children of God make Him happy; the irresponsible ones grieve His heart.

Determine

The dangerous situation in life to me is not the one of finding yourself in the lion's den, or in one more dreadful than that, but it is the situation of not knowing yourself—who you are, what you have, where you can go, and where you are going.

In researching the Adamic background, I was sorely grieved for the unresponsive heart and mind of Adam. Here was a man enormously empowered and given unrestrained authority, who chose not to live to his billing.

God did, and overdid, His part in the placement of Adam, and yet Adam blew it, as the following summary of what God did vivifies:

1. God is immortal, and He made Adam near immortal.
2. God is powerful, and He made Adam powerful.
3. Knowledge emanates from God, and therefore God thoroughly schooled Adam about who he is and what has been given to him (Gen 1:27–28).

Adam's sole reaction to his placement of power and authority was to determine. He was to determine the state and fate of every aspect of the created kingdom.

Adam's line of authority had such a broad a latitude that even after Eve had eaten the forbidden tree, he could have taken her though surgery to remove all those undesirable substances that had entered her out of her pleasurable trip into the forbidden tree. Adam failed because he refused to acknowledge who he was and what he had received. He was to rule by declarative determination. Declarative determination is the situation whereby the estate and outcome are decided by the stroke of words; and that marked the pinnacle of the Adamic authority.

To dress

Creation is a primary product. The secondary products on the mind of God were reserved for God's associate, man, to handle them. That was the primordial reason for the creation of the Adams.

God is a developmental God. He always builds on what He has started. His style had being to lay the foundation, and then provide humanity with the tools to build on the provided foundation:

> And the LORD God took the man, and put him into the garden of Eden to dress it and to keep it.
>
> —GENESIS 2:15

To keep

God is not a keeper, especially with things pertaining to humanity. What He produces, He gives humanity to keep it for Himself and on behalf of heaven (Gen. 2:15).

When Jesus Christ, Our Lord, was also departing, He requested the disciples to occupy till He cometh, via a parabolic entreaty:

> And he called his ten servants, and delivered them ten pounds, and said unto them, Occupy till I come.
>
> —Luke 19:13

And in consonance with the spirit and ideals of ministry we are to keep all the impartations of God to us—gifts, anointing, wisdom, and so on.

The principles of keeping

To every situation, there is an underlying principle. When the underlying principle to a situation is adhered to and applied forthwith, the sanctity and appreciation of that entity is safeguarded.

Contrary, if the underlying principle to an entity is flouted, there is the potential of the forfeiture, or lost of the entity. This dawned heavily on Adam

These were the underlying principles for the sanctity, appreciation, and perpetual keeping of the Garden of Eden:

1. Adam was to keep an eagle's eye on every development in the garden. (If he had done that, he would have spotted Satan before the devil encroached upon Eve.)
2. Adam was to monitor the growth of every tree, shrub, and flower in the garden for an immediate response of dressing.
3. Adam was to dress, and by dressing he would have added value to the garden.
4. In dressing the garden daily, Adam would have been so occupied that Satan could not have seen him idling to engage him polemically with regards to the tree of the knowledge of good and evil. Satan found an idle hand on Adam and opportunistically employed them.

The Hebrew word for keep—shamar

Shamar is from a primitive root that means "to hedge about (as with thorns)." If *shamar* were literally exegeted vis á vis Adam's response to the word, then there were more hard questions for Adam to answer:

1. Did Adam hedge about the Garden of Eden with thorns?
2. If Adam did hedge the Garden of Eden, how did Satan gain entrance to tempt him?

Analogizing the above with contemporary ministerial developments, do we have hedges around the gifts and the anointing of the Spirit we variously receive from the Holy Spirit? Do we have enough troubleshooting mechanisms to ward off modern-day, ministry-encroaching Satanists?

God gives us the gifts, the anointing, the wisdom, the knowledge, the skills, and the ministry to keep. Once He gives them He divests himself from ownership.

They essentially become our bona fide properties. However, God watcheth over everything He gives and demands accountability from us in consonance with His attribute.

He is the God of order, and therefore orderliness, which from another perspective is accountability, a divine attribute. In a way God "monkeys" our affairs in ministry to buttress the fact that ministry is essentially God's.

God is ministry. God is the Chief Minister. God owns ministry. God regulates ministry by calling, empowering, and commissioning the minister.

And ministry is the avenue through which God exerts His influence on earth, and executes His purpose for humanity through humanity. And it is from this perspective that the divine/human collaboration in ministry becomes imperative.

Ministry is ownership

God owns creation, and He also owns ministry, or in a broader perspective the church. Though God owns creation He does not dabble much in the affairs of creation.

He has left the destiny of creation to be governed by an established law with which He associated creation. God, however, deals differently with the church. He has established the church and He has left the ownership into the hand of the fivefold ministers on His behalf.

Every minister therefore owns his ministry on behalf of God. To this end the fivefold ministry was given to the ministers of God for them to experience some of the attributes of God experientially toward quality delivery.

Nothing, it is said, is broader than experience, and this extract from the erudite Geisler has some semblance of relevance to this:

> In this sense primary experience of God is the final court of appeal as to the genuineness of one's experience of God. Unless God were so experienced, there would be no valid basis for speaking of the reality or truth of that experience.[3]

> The ministry is yours, keep it.
> The ministry is yours, love it.
> The ministry is yours, nurture it.
> The ministry is yours, protect it.
> The ministry is yours, enliven it.
> The ministry is yours, guard it.
> And the ministry is yours, become committed to it.

God is committed to love hence creation, and its ultimate crown, humanity, to facilitate that love.

Ownership begets commitment

God is committed to man, hence his incarnation after the fall in order to redeem man. God is committed to man, hence the establishment of the church to consolidate his reunion with humanity. And God is so committed to humanity that He is spending endless time preparing a befitting place for them:

> Let not your heart be troubled: ye believe in God, believe also in me. In my Father's house are many mansions: if it were not so, I would have told you. I go to prepare a place for you.
>
> —John 14:1-2

Commitment is an indispensable feature in production and output, and great men and women in history never made it without commitment.

True ministers are seen by the commitment with which they carry out the ministry's agenda and purpose. Commitment is a conspicuous identity of any true and growing church. When ministers are committed, they are able to infest the membership with the virus of commitment. In this way the committed members of the church become committed to the pursuit of the goals and vision of the church.

When a minister is committed, and the members are committed, to the vision given to the church by God with the "Great Commission" as the anchor head, God becomes committed to such church.

The truth is this: God does not become committed to every church. This is not an automatic opener.

By the divine principle of output necessitates inputs, God only becomes committed to whoever becomes committed to Him. And the celebrated Rick Warren adds impetus to the overarching influence of commitment to the Christian vocation:

> Spiritual growth is intentional. It requires commitment and effort to grow. A person must want to grow, decide to grow, and make an effort to grow.[4]

MINISTRY IN THE POST-FALL ERA (O.T. CHURCH)

Theologically, the Jews were the Old Testament church. Therefore the symmetry between Old Testament unfoldings and events in the New Testament church, making the former playing the role of a harbinger to the latter, attest to the rehearsed divine order of humanity's redemption, reconciliation, and restoration to its source.

THE GENESIS OF THE OLD TESTAMENT CHURCH

The calling of Abraham from Iraq marked the beginning of the Old Testament church. After his calling, Abraham blossomed into such a giant figure that he is reckoned as the progenitor of the Old Testament, as well as the father of faith in the New Testament church.

GOD'S FIRST LEADERSHIP PRINCIPLE TO HUMANITY

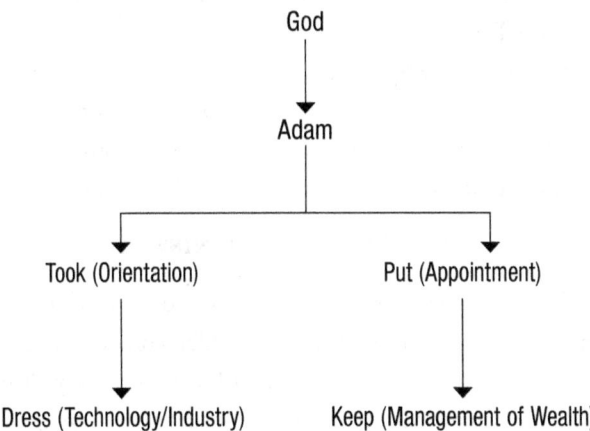

Chapter 8

THE FOCUS AND TARGET OF MINISTRY

FOCUS HAS A BROADER perspective and sphere of zooming while target is about specificity in a given focus area. It is within this hypothesis that we attempt to embark on this journey into the focus and target of ministry.

In creating, God had both a focus and a target. His focus was creation while man was His target. In the redemption voyage of Jesus Christ, to earth, He had both a focus and a target. His focus was to die for humanity, and His target was to redeem and reconcile them to the Father.

In the descent of the Holy Spirit to earth to commence the "pneumaic" ministry, He had a focus and a target in mind. The Holy Spirit's main focus of coming was the establishment of the church; and His target was the empowerment of the men and women in the church that had believed and confessed Jesus Christ as Lord and Savior.

THE FOCUS OF MINISTRY

Ministry is about a message from a personage (God), and this message has being chronicled and handed over to us per the Bible which comes to us essentially through the *logos*, and to a lesser extent from the *rhema*. (The *logos* is the written word, and the *rhema* is the revelation knowledge that comes to us from the *logos*.)

Thus the focus of ministry becomes the Word through which we see God and know Him; and also see and know ourselves better in order to have a full and clearer grasp of our calling into the ministry.

Without seeing, knowing, and having God; and without seeing and knowing ourselves better via the redemptive process, we cannot be in ministry.

Ministry is about God through us, the born anew, hence the need to know Him before we can articulate His wishes through us. And 1 Corinthians 2:16 is the quintessence of the above argument:

> For who has known the mind of the Lord that he may instruct him? but we have the mind of Christ.

The Incarnate Word as focus of ministry

Jesus Christ is our example in ministry, and He doubles as the facsimile representation of the Triune God in the flesh. The incarnation was God in the flesh, in man, and among men:

> To wit, that God was in Christ, reconciling the world unto himself, not imputing their trespasses unto them; and hath committed unto us the word of reconciliation.
> —2 Corinthians 5:19

In the light of the above, the incarnate Christ, the living Jesus, should be the focus of ministry. For it is only in Him, through Him, and by Him that we have any idea of who God is, how God is, and why God is.

Without Jesus Christ, we are out of contact with the radar of divinity, and once we are bereft of this, any idea of ministry loses its focus and becomes an illusion.

Jesus is our Savior, and our primary response to faith is our salvation. Jesus is our example, and our secondary response to faith is our calling into ministry. Consequently, the amalgam of the above offers a purview of the overriding impact of focus unveiled in Hebrews 12:2:

> Looking unto Jesus the author and finisher of our faith; who for the joy that was set before him endured the cross, despising the shame, and is set down at the right hand of the throne of God.

When the living Christ becomes your focus in ministry, you can endure your own cross in ministry. Every calling of God has an attendant cross, and every attendant cross of our calling has a "Golgotha" which when fulfilled offers opportunities to receive crowns commensurate to one's calling and performance thereto.

Then when the living Christ becomes your focus in ministry, you can despise the shame associated with ministry as your focus on Him assuredly offers soothing balms to the associated pains and anguish of ministry.

Some enter ministry with the focus on fame. Other enter ministry with the focus on wealth. And again some are carried away by their insatiable ego into ministry in order to build a "tower of Babel" for it through ministry. In ministry there is no "tower of Babel" for pride and ego.

People in these brackets in ministry do not have any foundation to stand on in ministry. And as such, any wind of challenge, wind of obstacle, and wind of frustration that come their way puts them down en route to annihilation in ministry.

In ministry, our focus on the incarnate Christ who is seated on the greatest seat of authority in heaven becomes our greatest foundation.

Jesus Christ himself had a focus while here on earth, otherwise He would not have been able to carry the cross to Calvary and endure those agonizing moments of excruciating pain. The Father was His focus. And once He focused on the Father, He received strength from the One who sent Him.

In ministry, one must know and acknowledge that he or she is called and sent by a higher Being. He who called you and sent you has His integrity at stake in your calling. When you succeed and excel in your calling, His name is glorified, but when you misconduct yourself via His name it casts a slur on His integrity.

To focus on the incarnate Christ in ministry, you must make Him count and make yourself not count. You must let Him take all the glories associated with your calling while taking all the ignominies associated with your calling. Those are hard facts, but it is the indubitable truth!

To focus on the incarnate Christ, you must always look to heaven and not to the earth in your ministry pursuits. The atmospheric heaven and the earth with their unfoldings try to unsettle and unmake us in ministry, but eyes glued on the seated and established Christ on high, above the atmospheric heaven and the second heaven, bring assurance and calmed nerves that drown the above into oblivion.

Our focus on the risen Christ not only brings Christ to the purview of our spiritual senses, but we are also graciously enabled to catch glimpses of the galaxy of angelic hosts who minister to us, as well as the contented faces of the innumerable company of great witnesses that surround the throne of the enthroned Christ.

> Wherefore seeing we also are compassed about with so great a cloud of witnesses, let us lay aside every weight, and the sin which doth so easily beset us, and let us run with patience the race that is set before us.
> —Hebrews 12:1

The written Word as focus of ministry

Jesus Christ, the Son of God and the second Being in the Trinity, has manifested Himself to humanity in three forms:

1. Through the Incarnation
2. Through the written Word
3. Through the spoken Word

As the Incarnate God, Jesus Christ was flawless, and was also authoritative, so He could be the source of inspirational to others.

And as the written Word, the Holy Spirit has breathed on Him to maintain the same level of inspiration He offered to the pioneer disciples who were graciously enabled to walk, eat, and sleep with the Lord.

Without doubt, the written Word is both the Christian's and ministry's greatest source of reference as well as inspiration. The Word informs. The Word leads. The Word inspires. And the Word comforts. On inspiration, Paul underscores its importance and centrality to humanity, especially Christendom, via 2 Timothy 3:16–17:

> All scripture is given by inspiration of God, and is profitable for doctrine, for reproof, for correction, for instruction in righteousness: That the man of God may be perfect, thoroughly furnished unto all good works.

The power that oozed from the Incarnate Word while He was with the pioneer disciples does the same to people that are associated with Jesus Christ through the written Word.

Jesus' power that manifested through the incarnate Word manifests the same through the written Word as applied, affirmed, and enforced by its adherents. The power in the written Word is not devalued as against the Incarnate Word.

Through the written Word, we have both the historicity and the personage of the total Christ. When we look to the written Word for inspiration, we are caught into the presence of both the Father and Jesus, seated on the great throne in heaven and stretching to us their hands of strength to strengthen our feeble limbs in ministry.

And David, a great beneficiary of the principle of focusing on the Lord, says it experientially in Psalm 16:8:

> I have set the LORD always before me: because he is at my right hand, I shall not be moved.

When you focus on Christ, you are unconsciously telling Him that He is your guide. And in this way this comment by the highly erudite church administrator Rick Warren becomes pertinent:

> Whenever God guides, He provides.[5]

Today's Christian church worker is better placed in terms of evaluating and appraising Christ than the people that physically walked and worked with Christ.

Through the written Word we have a biography of Jesus Christ, especially through the Gospels which offer us an opportunity for a consistent telescopic evaluation and analysis of the Messianic ministry.

Today we have the whole Bible with us; and more than that, the different editions of it give us vast insight into the personage and ministry of our Lord and Savior Jesus Christ, our model and mentor in ministry.

Today through the written Word we are graciously favored to be able to study Christ better, for a better knowledge of His personage, a better understanding of His actions, and a deeper insight into the underlying principles that catapulted Him into fame.

Jesus has promised us through John 12:12 that if we believe in Him we shall be able to replicate the acts that He produced in ministry. But in the desire to fulfill this promise, a mere wish for its fulfillment becomes wishful thinking.

Every promise in the Bible requires the application of an analogue principle to make the promise potent and feasible. Once we are able to unravel the principles associated with the promises, Jesus becomes real as though He were present.

In the written Word we are offered knowledge of and insight into the holistic personage of Jesus Christ.

The spoken/prophetic word as focus of ministry

God the Father spoke. He spoke to Adam personally, and later spoke through the prophets after the fall of humanity.

God the Son spoke; and for Him, He did it personally as this extract purveys:

> Then came the officers to the chief priests and Pharisees; and they said unto them, Why have ye not brought him? The officers answered, Never man spake like this man.
>
> —John 7:45–46

Then God the Holy Spirit spoke, and now speaks. He spoke through the pioneer disciples and continues to speak to humanity through the ministry of prophecy and through homilies delivered across the length and breadth of the world by men and women who are His carriers and couriers.

Inferentially, carriers and couriers of the Holy Spirit are people who are filled by the Holy Spirit and those who allow His influence to have a greater influence over their human inclinations during the preparations and delivery of homilies.

The spoken word becomes a major focus of ministry from the perspective that men and women called into ministry are called primarily to preach. And to preach you must speak words, and these words invariably qualify to be tagged either the Spoken Word or the spoken word.

The latter, spoken word, becomes the spoken word of humanity if the word preached is bereft of divine unction and power, while the former Spoken Word becomes the near Spoken Word of God if the word spoken or preached is laden with divine unction and power.

People whose preaching word becomes the Spoken Word of God are people whose lives have been nurtured and shaped by the Holy Spirit.

People whose preaching word enables listeners to become enriched and experience the impact of a Spoken Word are those who have through the Word of God been crucified and are resurrected into a new form of life by the Holy Spirit. These are a rare breed; they are people with the experiential "experience," aspiring to be in the shoes of Paul who in the climax of this experience says:

> I am crucified with Christ: nevertheless I live; yet not I, but Christ liveth in me: and the life which I now live in the flesh I live by the faith of the Son of God, who loved me, and gave himself for me.
> —Galatians 2:20

To such people their focus is the Spoken Word; consequently, they die to self in order to make the word preached relive the virtues and traits of the Spoken Word of God.

To such people everything is secondary except the Spoken Word; and thus they "eat" the Word, "drink" the Word, and "sleep" the Word to bring to fruition its power and impact.

The Target of Ministry

Every purpose is geared toward a goal, and every aspiration has a destination. To this end the target becomes the definer of both purpose and aspiration.

If great accomplishers in history had practiced archery, they would have become all-time great hitters. Why? Great accomplishers undoubtedly are people who hit their dream targets of life.

Every dream and every vision is the target of life, and once you hit the center spot of your dream or vision, you are there.

The target therefore must become the revolving factor of our lives, and on this the celebrated Rick Warren shares a thought relative to consistency in preaching style:

> You cannot switch back and forth between targeting seekers and believers in the same services.[6]

The Lost—the Primary Target of Ministry

Each member within the Trinity had a ministry, and with their respective ministries, man was the hub. The Father God's ministry was creation and its governance, and that man was the target. The Son God's descent to Earth via the incarnation was to epitomize the practicality of ministry, and for that humanity's salvation was the target.

The Spirit God, as the "anchorman" in the Trinity, came down in full personage, and power to actualize and concretize the "Calvaryic" ideals, and for him too, the church which has humanity as its mainstay was the focus.

Indisputably then, the lost, the perishing, the unsaved, the people outside the "Commonwealth of Israel" become the target of ministry.

And Luke 19:10 undoubtedly fits for selection in buttressing the point that the lost is the primary target of ministry:

> For the Son of man is come to seek and to save that which was lost.

Great ministries and great churches are led by leaders with the penchant for the lost, and for this reason their focus and target are primarily on those without their "nets" and not on those already in the "net."

And again in this instant, the man reputed to be one of the greatest thinkers in the church today is our port of call for augmenting this point:

> Each week at Saddleback, we remind ourselves who we are trying to reach: Saddleback Sam and his wife Samantha. Once you know your target, it will determine many of the components of your seeker service: music style, message topics, testimonies, creative arts and much more.[7]

Any church or ministry which has the lost as the primary target creates a seeker-sensitive atmosphere which climaxes into a seeker-sensitive service.

Under such a milieu, members will invite their friends week after week, and the ministry will experience a steady influx of unchurched visitors that ultimately add to the numbers that help to grow a larger church.

In such churches and ministries diversity and variety are very profound in their ministrations, be it worship, message, or human relationship. They blend the conservative ideals with the emerging contemporaneous stuffs.

The following tabulated features are visibly infectious at their meetings:

- The service is made as easy as possible to attend.
- There is marked difference in the pace and flow of service.
- The music is fluid and activating.
- The entire worship service is uplifting.
- The service is bereft of extensive technicalities.
- The environment is brightened to add life and give more meaning to ministry.

- There is reality in the service.

Preparing the Saved for the Work of Ministry— the Secondary Target of Ministry

Winning the lost is difficult, but preparing the saved for the work of ministry to me is more difficult.

Relative to this development our Lord gave the fivefold ministries in Ephesians 4:11: 1) for equipping God's people for works of service (4:12); and 2) for the spiritual growth and development of the body of Christ as God intended (4:13–16).

Going for the lost is like attacking the enemy while preparing the saved, for the work of ministry is like defending the church. These are the hallmarks of a total church: it must be able to attack, and it must be able to defend at the same time by the caliber of personnel in its arsenals.

The fivefold ministries are the topmost posts in the church, and as such the Lord painstakingly prepared a conducive ground to assuage any of the devil's tricks:

> Wherefore he saith, When he ascended up on high, he led captivity captive, and gave gifts unto men….And he gave some, apostles; and some, prophets; and some, evangelists; and some, pastors and teachers.
> —Ephesians 4:8, 11

For the church to become solid rock, the fivefold ministries would have to work in tandem on the members to ensure spiritual growth, maturity, and commitment.

Becoming like Christ is the result of the efforts and commitment we make, but these are bolstered by the teachings, guidance, and encouragement we get from our leaders in the fivefold ministries.

God's desire, which must be articulated by the church, is for its sons and daughters to grow but not to remain spiritual runts after salvation. Being a spiritual runt defeats the purpose of the new birth.

To this end the fivefold ministries lay the fundamental framework, and the laity is expected to respond appropriately with the spiritual exercises to grow and mature thereby, as this analogy seeks to underscore:

> Anyone can become physically fit if he or she will regularly do certain exercises and practice good health habits. Likewise, spiritual fitness is simply a matter of learning certain spiritual exercises and being disciplined to do them until they become habits.[8]

The avenue to Christian growth is two-pronged—relationship with God and fellowship with the brethren. We relate to God through the Word—obedience, promises, and application of its principles.

We fellowship with the brethren through church attendance and affiliation with the various ministries in the church and the opportunities they offer to be in ministry within the church and without the church.

Preparing the Saints for the Rapture—the Ultimate Target of Ministry

Every journey has a beginning, and everything with a beginning definitely has an end. This axiom is also relative to the Christian life or the journey of Christianity. It begins when you are born again after you accept Jesus Christ as your Lord and personal Savior, and it ends when we are raptured to heaven to begin a new life of eternity with the Trinity.

To this extent the Rapture becomes relevant to the treatise being addressed. Consequently, the Rapture becomes the ultimate target of ministry, for after all, if ministry wins the lost and adequately prepares them for the work of ministry without climaxing their preparation en route to heaven via the rapture, it would not have done a holistic job.

The term *Rapture*

The term *Rapture* is derived from the Latin word *reptus*, which means "caught away" or "caught up." This Latin word is equivalent to the Greek *harpazō*, translated as "caught up" in 1 Thessalonians 4:17.

The description of this event in 1 Corinthians 15 refers to the catching up of the church from the earth to meet the Lord in the air.

The hope that our Savior will soon return to take us out of the world to "ever be with the Lord" (1 Thess. 4:17) is the blessed hope of all the redeemed (Titus 2:13). Dr. Dwight Pentecost throws more light on this eschatological unfolding:

> The Lord promised to prepare a place for His own. At the rapture and resurrection of the church the saints of this age are, after judgment and marriage, installed in that prepared place.[9]

The nearness and expectation of the Rapture strengthens us when we are pressed down from all directions in our pursuit of ministry ideals. Ministry is so demanding that, except for the hope of heaven via the Rapture, many enfeebled limbs would have thrown in the towel midstream in ministry. But the Rapture is so reassuring, so comforting, and so consolatory that it whittles into oblivion the pain and anguish we experience in ministry.

And it is in this perspective that these reassuring words of Paul are my capstone choice in this instance:

> I have fought a good fight, I have finished my course, I have kept the faith: Henceforth there is laid up for me a crown of righteousness, which the Lord, the righteous judge, shall give me at that day: and not to me only, but unto all them also that love his appearing.
>
> —2 Timothy 4:7–8

The promise of heaven is so real and so good that some have traded their lives for it. The Rapture, which is the ultimate target of ministry, must become the pivot of ministry—of homily, evangelism, worship, and all else.

When Rapture consciousness dominates ministry, people in the pews will count all things but dung for the knowledge of the excellency of Christ. In this way our Christian conviction will soar beyond the skyscrapers. The church today is filled with people with weak conviction. Once weak convicted people fill the church, we will not have people willing and ready to die for the cause of Christ.

Achievers—people who have made the greatest impact on this world, either for good or for evil—are not necessarily the smartest or wealthiest people. They are people who have changed the face of the world because of their convictions.

And it is said that in 1943 over 100,000 young people went berserk in the then world's largest stadium in Munich, chanting, "Hitler, we are yours." Their commitment allowed them to conquer Europe.

The Great Commission is moving at a snail's pace primarily due to the absence of fire in Christendom. And how will there be fire if conviction is a forgotten word within theological and ecclesiastical circles?

Chapter 9

THE APOSTLE

The Branches of Ministry (Fivefold Ministry Gifts)

THERE ARE TWO MAIN foundations upon which the church is built. These foundations are those of the apostles and the prophets, and Ephesians 2:20 brings their significance to bear on this treatise:

And are built upon the foundation of the apostles and prophets.

And then the second half of Ephesians 2:20 brings solidity to the structures as Jesus comes to the scene:

Jesus Christ himself being the chief corner stone.

Although there are five major players in the fivefold ministry, only two—the apostle and the prophet—are mentioned as being the foundations upon which we are built. This underscores the indispensable roles they play and underlines the strategic position and influence they bring to bear on the governance of the church.

Every structure that is not supported by a solid rock foundation cannot stand beyond a generation, much less eternity. The church, however, has stood for over two thousand years, having gone through an avalanche of tirades and attacks. With Jesus as the chief cornerstone, and with the apostles and prophets complementing admirably as dependable foundations, the size and strength of the church keeps increasing. And this axiom finds room in the candid observation of Rick Warren relative to foundation and growth:

The foundation determines both the size and the strength of a building. You can never build larger than the foundation can handle.[1]

THE TERM *APOSTLE*

The title "apostle" is applied to certain leaders in the New Testament. *Apostle* is the noun form, and the verb form *apostello* means "to send someone on a special mission as a messenger, a personal representative, and in some instances a pioneer." The title is used for Christ (Heb. 3:1):

> Wherefore, holy brethren, partakers of the heavenly calling, consider the Apostle and High Priest of our profession, Christ Jesus.

And the twelve disciples follow suit in Matthew 10:2:

> Now the names of the twelve apostles are these; The first, Simon, who is called Peter, and Andrew his brother; James the son of Zebedee, and John his brother

Then Paul, the man whose apostleship occupies an integral position in the church's administration, organization, and functionality comes next via Romans 1:1:

> Paul, a servant of Jesus Christ, called to be an apostle, separated unto the gospel of God.

The strategic position of the apostle is seen within the perspective that he is the chief policy maker of the church. The physical policy framework, the organization, and the administration of the church are largely influenced by the direction of the apostle.

In consonance with the traditions of apostleship, the contemporary apostle should not be a novice, but should be someone who is a seasoned and time-tested leader and one who has gone through the gritty battles associated with church leadership.

And a couple of verses from Paul's spiritual qualifications for overseer will suffice:

> Not a novice, lest being lifted up with pride he fall into the condemnation of the devil. Moreover he must have a good report of them which are without; lest he fall into reproach and the snare of the devil.
> —1 TIMOTHY 3:6–7

In a broader sense we have three types of apostles: the pioneer apostle, the representative apostle, and the messenger apostle.

THE EARLY PIONEER APOSTLES

Apostleship takes its roots from the pioneer apostles who were handpicked and groomed in the Word by Jesus, and later empowered by the Holy Spirit to begin the church.

Two marked developments unfolded before their commissioning into ministry: 1) they were prepared in the Word for knowledge, and 2) they were prepared by the Holy Spirit in power. These two developments become the benchmark for apostleship.

The pioneer apostles were men who manifested extraordinary spiritual leadership, were anointed with power to confront directly the powers of darkness and to confirm the gospel with miracles, and were dedicated to establishing churches according to apostolic truth and purity.

They were itinerate, risking their lives for the name of our Lord Jesus Christ and the advancement of the gospel, as Acts 11:19 affirms:

> Now they which were scattered abroad upon the persecution that arose about Stephen travelled as far as Phenice, and Cyprus, and Antioch, preaching the word to none but unto the Jews only.

THE CONTEMPORARY PIONEER APOSTLE

As the name connotes, the contemporary pioneer apostle is an apostle called by God, enhanced in knowledge, and empowered and tutored by the Spirit to take on the adventurous ministry of going to "barren lands" where the gospel has never being preached or churches planted to preach, teach, plant, and nourish.

The nature of ministry of the contemporary apostle is homologous to that of the early pioneer apostles, and as such those in this apostleship must be men and women deeply encapsulated in the Word and in the Spirit.

Pioneer apostleship is not tea-party apostleship; it is risk-taking apostleship. Pioneer apostleship is the apostolic office where the normal duties and ministry of an apostle are carried out, most often in the company of believers.

The risk-taking apostleship is one where the apostolic duties and ministries are shrouded in life-threatening and life-taking dangers. All, save John, among the twelve pioneer apostles perished, illustrating the absolute dangers associated with this office. Some moments before Paul was murdered, he exclaimed:

> For I am now ready to be offered, and the time of my departure is at hand.
> I have fought a good fight, I have finished my course, I have kept the faith.
> —2 TIMOTHY 4:6–7

Contemporary pioneer apostles go to where probably no one has gone, and they adapt to the culture of the new environments in which they find themselves, if their mission is to have any impact in the lives of the people to whom they minister.

Pioneer apostles, for the sake of Christ, have to learn to eat the food that their hosts eat; change their dressing code to their host's dressing code; and to some extent reorient their psyche to suit their new environment toward cooperation, collaboration, and consensus.

It becomes an issue of "if you want to win us, you must live like we live." If you are a pioneer apostle from a Western country on a mission to a heathenish country, you cannot get results painting yourself in Western cultural practices. You either reorient your culture to the culture of the hosts or pack your bags and return home.

In summation, the pioneer apostle is inextricably involved in the spiritual, mental, and physical lives of the people they attempt to reach for Jesus.

The Messenger Apostle

The messenger apostle is one who goes from one area to another on short trips to give apostolic insight and direction to local community church leaders.

The ministry of the messenger apostle takes on the cloak of apologetics. In this direction they tend to safeguard the Christian standards that have been bequeathed to us by the pioneer apostle as is stated in Jude 1:3:

> Beloved, when I gave all diligence to write unto you of the common salvation, it was needful for me to write unto you, and exhort you that ye should earnestly contend for the faith which was once delivered unto the saints.

The other important ministry of the messenger apostle has to do with administrative empowerment. By administrative empowerment the visiting messenger apostle ordains and commissions emerging young ministers who do not come under the umbrella of any church into the various ministries of their calling.

This development is very visible in developing countries where the gospel is spreading at an alarming rate, culminating in the springing up of many churches.

The snag in this second ministry of the messenger apostle is that most often these licensed independent church leaders tend to be aloof with ministry discipline and standards that invariably affect the honor and dignity associated with the ministers of the gospel.

The Representative Apostle

The representative apostleship is relative to episcopacy. By this the representative apostle is the most senior minister who is sent by the church to oversee a number of churches and ministers in a given geographical location. The representative apostle is most often an experienced minister, one who is a team player, and who is also able to inspire younger ministers to realize their full potential in ministry.

The representative apostleship is very prevalent in many developing countries where there are large denominational churches under centralized administration. The following is a tabulated summary of the duties of the representative apostle:

1. General oversight of churches assigned to his jurisdiction.

2. To liaise between the headquarters of his church and the churches and ministers in the said location.
3. To maintain order and discipline within the fraternity of the various ministries in each branch or assembly of the church.
4. To select potential ministers in his area of jurisdiction for training and calling into the ministry.
5. To ensure the upgrading of the financial gains of the churches in the areas where he presides.
6. To hold periodic retreats and seminars for the branch pastors, elders, deacons, and deaconesses to ensure unity and cohesiveness of the various ministries within the church.

GRAPH OF A DENOMINATIONAL CHURCH STRUCTURE UNDER A CENTRALIZED ADMINISTRATION RELATIVE TO THE REPRESENTATIVE APOSTLE

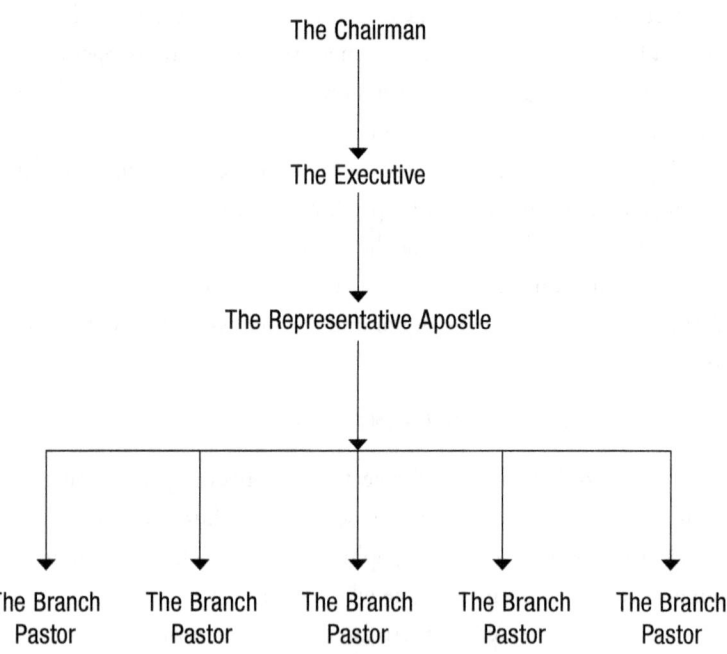

Chapter 10

THE PROPHET

The Branches of Ministry (Fivefold Ministry Gifts)

THE PROPHETIC MINISTRY, FROM the theological perspective, is a broad-spectrum menu for mass enjoyment, but from the technical diaphragm it is one for the coterie of experts.

Inferentially, the mass enjoyment component of the prophetic ministry is simply that every Christian who takes the Word of God to his neighbor as enjoined by the Great Commission is unfolding a prophetic message, for the Word takes on a strong cloak of prophecy.

Then the second element of the prophetic ministry as one fit for the coterie of experts just paints the professional picture of this diverse and varied ministry.

PROPHETS—WHO THEY ARE

Prophets are men or women in the church who speak under the direct impulse of the Holy Spirit, and their main motivation and concern is the spiritual life and purity of the church. They were, and are, raised up and empowered by the Holy Spirit to bring a message from God to His people:

> And finding disciples, we tarried there seven days: who said to Paul through the Spirit, that he should not go up to Jerusalem.
> —ACTS 21:4

PROPHETS—THEIR FUNCTION

The prophet's function within the church includes the following:

- He is a Spirit-filled proclaimer and interpreter of the Word of God, called by God to warn, exhort, comfort, and edify. The main function of the prophet, though, is to proclaim and interpret both the *logos* word and the *rhema* word.

- He exercises the gift of prophecy.
- He is at times a seer who foretells the future (1 Chron. 29:29; Acts 11:28, 21:10–11).

Prophets—Their Character

Prophets have a strong apologetic character, and thus their burden, desire, and ability include:

- A zeal for church purity (John 17:15–17; 1 Cor. 6:9–11).
- A deep sensitivity to evil and the capacity to identify, define, and hate unrighteousness (Rom. 12:9; Heb. 1:9).
- An inherent dependence on the Word of God to validate his message (Luke 4:17–19; 1 Cor. 15:3–4).

Prophets—Their Message

The prophet's message during the Old Testament dispensation was very authoritative and had a near infallible status. However, in this New Testament dispensation, when the Word became flesh and was chronicled in the Bible which is now accessible to all, the near infallible stature and absolute authority of the prophet's message has ceased as pinpointed here in Hebrews 1:1–2:

> God, who at sundry times and in divers manners spake in time past unto the fathers by the prophets, Hath in these last days spoken unto us by his Son, whom he hath appointed heir of all things, by whom also he made the worlds.

This therefore puts the prophet's message under microscopic observation and evaluation by the church, other prophets, and the Word of God.

Indeed, the Word of God becomes the "last professor" in this chain of observers and evaluators when it comes to assessing their message. As this scripture indicates, others should judge the message of the prophet by the Word:

> Let the prophets speak two or three, and let the other judge.
> —1 Corinthians 14:29

And also, the congregation is required to discern and test whether the prophet's witness is from God (1 Cor. 14:29; 1 John 4:1).

Prophets—Their Importance to the Church

The prophet is one of the main pillars of the church, structurally and spiritually. The prophet and the apostle constitute the two essential pillars on which stands the church's foundation, which has as a cornerstone the Lord Jesus Christ Himself:

> And are built upon the foundation of the apostles and prophets, Jesus Christ himself being the chief corner stone.
> —Ephesians 2:20

By the strategic placement of the prophet and the supplementary role he plays to the apostolic office, the prophet's importance to the church is seen primarily in the spiritual leadership and direction he gives to the church.

A church with good prophetic leadership never goes blind when there is the need for a strictly spiritual direction outside the Word of God. This development is essentially acute in places like Africa and where the church is under constant siege by an avalanche of demonic forces.

A church that rejects God's prophets will be a declining church drifting toward worldliness and the compromise of biblical truth and standards (1 Cor. 14:3; Matt. 23:31–38).

Any time prophets are around, people in the church are very particular when compromising with Christian standards for fear of being exposed by the prophet through the Holy Spirit, as evidenced in the unfortunate incident of Ananias in Acts 5:3, 5:

> But Peter said, Ananias, why hath Satan filled thine heart to lie to the Holy Ghost, and to keep back part of the price of the land?...And Ananias hearing these words fell down, and gave up the ghost: and great fear came on all them that heard these things.

A ministry of the Word without supernatural signs accompanying it makes the podium dry and tends to project God only as a rhetorical personality.

Yes, God spoke and continues to speak, but He is known best as the One who is ultimate in power and infinite in wisdom. When the Word became incarnated, His ministry was a quintessence of both the spoken Word and the miracle Word. Jesus preached and taught in consonance with the spoken Word; He healed after preaching and teaching in affirmation of the miracle Word.

Even in prayer, one sometimes needs a spiritual direction akin to the prophetic ministry in order to get the desired results.

If the spoken Word is not backed by the miracle Word, or if the miracle Word is not followed by the ministry of the spoken Word, the Messianic ministry which we are graciously co-opted into is robbed of its holistic garment.

It thus becomes imperative that the apostolic ministry, which has a strong leaning on the spoken Word, is supplemented by the prophetic ministry, which comes in with empirical proof of the power of the Word via the supernatural that accompanies it.

The Three Prophetic Personalities

There are three identities within the prophetic personalities just as there are three steps within the prophetic structures of the prophetic ministry. First, the three prophetic personalities are addressed. These three personalities are:

1. The Nazarene prophet
2. The prophet of grace
3. The prophet of the fulfillment of the prophetic calling

The Nazarene Prophet

The Nazarene prophet is a prophet of the highest standards, hence Jesus' association with Nazareth as His birthplace (although in fairness to biblical and theological truth, He was the incarnate God in the flesh).

The Nazarene prophet is a prophet of the womb. With being a prophet of the womb inferentially comes the association of the Nazarene prophet with certain pietistic requirements that impact either positively or negatively on their personage or the purpose by which they were called.

Two essential features separate the Nazarene prophet from the other two prophetic identities: the Nazarene covenant and the Nazarene vow.

The Nazarene covenant

The Nazarene covenant associated with the Nazarene prophet is relative to the principle that "to whom much is given much is expected." When God gives you more, He certainly expects more output.

In ministry, the bigger the gift and the stronger the anointing imparted upon a person, the more God expects from him or her by way of delivery.

By the Nazarene covenant God enters into a covenant with the Nazarene prophet, either personally or with the parents, who are enjoined to inform their child the terms of the covenant in order to make it as though it was entered in personally with the child. Judges 13:5, which refers to the birth and ministry of Samson, is reflective of this:

> For lo, thou shalt conceive, and bear a son; and no razor shall come on his head: for the child shall be a Nazarite unto God from the womb: and he shall begin to deliver Israel out of the hand of the Philistines.

Jeremiah is another prophet whose calling has some semblance of a Nazarene. Jeremiah's prophetic calling, although it never had any Nazarene covenantal attachment, was however initiated from the womb, akin to the Samsonic calling, the quintessence of the Nazarene calling:

> Before I formed thee in the belly I knew thee; and before thou camest forth out of the womb I sanctified thee, and I ordained thee a prophet unto the nations.
> —JEREMIAH 1:5

Samuel, one of the greatest prophets in the history of Israel and to a large extent the church, is our last reference point in this treatise. Samuel was a man who satisfied all the Nazarene benchmarks for prophets and lived to the billing of the Nazarene prophet.

And unlike Samson, who did not live to satisfy all the requirements of the Nazarene standard, Samuel did, by his absolute separation, absolute consecration, and absolute devotion to God. First Samuel 8:4–5 is corroborative:

> Then all the elders of Israel gathered themselves together, and came to Samuel unto Ramah, And said unto him, Behold, thou art old, and thy sons walk not in thy ways: now make us a king to judge us like all the nations.

As mentioned earlier regarding the standards of the Nazarene prophet, this also serves as the demarcation line between that breed of prophet and the prophets from the other two remaining stocks.

Separation, consecration, and absolute devotion are the marks, mainstay, and cutting edge of the Nazarene prophet. Once these were abused, downplayed, or treated with irreverence, the office became a bygone entity.

The Nazarene vow

The Nazarene vow is one undertaken, either by the parent of a prospective Nazarene prophet or by the person himself, for a totally separated lifelong ministry to God.

Samuel came under scrutiny under the Nazarene covenant, but he also fits to be treated under the Nazarene vow as well, per the intonation of his mother prior to his birth, recounted in 1 Samuel 1:11:

> And she vowed a vow, and said, O LORD of hosts, if thou wilt indeed look on the affliction of thine handmaid, and remember me, and not forget

thine handmaid, but wilt give unto thine handmaid a man child, then I will give him unto the LORD all the days of his life, and there shall no razor come upon his head.

The essence or impact of Samuel's mother's vow was dualistic, relative to the Nazarene vow. Both "No razor shall come upon his head" and "I will give him unto the Lord all the days of his life" come under the Nazarene vow.

THE PROPHET OF GRACE

From a general theological perspective, grace is reckoned as unmerited favor, and its Grecian source *charis,* which is defined as "graciousness," unveils the word.

The prophet of grace is a prophet God calls into the prophetic family to portray the grace of God through the prophetic ministry to people. The ministry of the prophet of grace is especially pronounced in Africa, where so many come under various demonic attacks and dislocation of purposes that except for the ministry of these prophets, much harm would have been caused to the people of God.

Indeed most of the office holders of the prophet of grace are unlearned and so theologically deficient that their ministry is quickly discernible and traceable to the gracious divine hand and power in operation.

Jonah comes to mind in this instance. Some scholars opine that Jonah was the son of the widow of Zarephath whom Elijah raised from the dead. If this were so, then he was the man God used to manifest His great mercy and grace to the sinful people of Nineveh.

So then Jonah became a beneficiary of grace in order to become the vehicle of grace for God. This is the hallmark of the prophet of grace; he is graciously called to graciously manifest the grace of God.

THE PROPHET OF THE FULFILLMENT OF THE PROPHETIC CALLING

Prophets of the fulfillment of the prophetic calling are people who invoke the tenet and spirit of Matthew 11:12:

> And from the days of John the Baptist until now the kingdom of heaven suffereth violence, and the violent take it by force.

By the invocation of the tenet and the spirit of Matthew 11:12 inferentially is that these are people who took the Word of God as it is, believed in the promises of God, and by faith prayed for the prophetic gift, received it, and began to function like prophets with all rights and privileges within the prophetic enclave.

The things of God, including the gifts, are accessed through prayer. This means that there is a realm in which are deposited the things of God. This realm is within the location of the geographical location of heaven. When one's intense prayer gets to heaven and finds itself in a specific zone in the realm where certain gifts are accessible, these gifts find their way to the pray-er.

This second breed of prophets in this enclave could be labeled prophets who pay the price of initiation into the prophetic office. These are prophets who pursue a closer walk with God; who go deeper in relationship with God than the average Christian would go; and who subject their passion, their desire, their affection, and their inclination to the control of God in order to climax in their divine-human relationship.

To these people, the unction and other virtues of the Trinity come upon them voluntarily and unconsciously, and without notice they find themselves as different people being moved by the Spirit of God.

To these people the Spirit prepares and moves in and with them even before the ceremonial human anointing is initiated. God anoints them indoors before He makes it official with the ceremonial anointing as evidenced in the life of David in 1 Samuel 16:13:

> Then Samuel took the horn of oil, and anointed him in the midst of his brethren: and the Spirit of the LORD came upon David from that day forward. So Samuel rose up, and went to Ramah.

The name of the affable Joshua also comes up for picks in enhancing this hypothesis. For years Joshua braced the odds, going through challenges and dangers in serving Moses, his master and God's instrument of human leadership in the Exodus.

And in appreciation of Joshua's servitude and incomparable loyalty, God awarded him an office which is an amalgam of the acme of political and spiritual office, the president, and the prophet of Israel to take the Israelites to the Promised Land:

> Now after the death of Moses the servant of the LORD it came to pass, that the LORD spake unto Joshua the son of Nun, Moses' minister, saying, Moses my servant is dead; now therefore arise, go over this Jordan, thou, and all this people, unto the land which I do give to them, even to the children of Israel.
>
> —JOSHUA 1:1–2

In summation, prophets of the fulfillment of the prophetic calling pay the price for this office. They do not enjoy the privilege of the prophetic office through the arm of grace, but through the arm of fulfillment of the requirements for this office.

The Three Steps Within the Prophetic Ladder

The prophetic ministry is a very progressive one, and the three steps within the prophetic ladder only amplify the progressive nature of this exciting and challenging arm within the fivefold ministry.

The three steps within the prophetic ladder are:

1. Gift of prophecy
2. Ministry of prophecy
3. Office of the prophet

The gift of prophecy

The gift of prophecy is the foundational stratum in the prophetic enclave. That means to say that the gift of prophecy is in most cases the first gift one gets in the prophetic family en route to full-blown prophetic ministry.

The gift of prophecy is a spirit of inspiration that comes on a person in the church to speak uplifting words of exhortation and comfort to people in the household of faith. A person operating under the gift of prophecy, or from another perspective under the spirit of prophecy, does not do so by hearing from God before transmitting the message to the hearers, but only speaks by inspiration when the spirit of prophecy comes on him or her.

The gift or spirit of prophecy, aside from being a foundational gift in the prophetic family, is also a mass gift usable by everyone in the congregation living right in the Word and with the Spirit:

> For ye may all prophesy one by one, that all may learn, and all may be comforted.
>
> —1 Corinthians 14:31

We must distinguish between prophecy in 1 Corinthians 12:10 as a temporary manifestation of the Spirit from prophecy cited as a ministry gift of the church in Ephesians 4:11. As a ministry gift, prophecy is given only to some mature leaders who must then function as prophets with all rights and privileges within the church in consonance with Ephesians 2:20:

> And are built upon the foundation of the apostles and prophets, Jesus Christ himself being the chief corner stone.

Prophecy is not the delivery of a previously prepared sermon from the person who is the vehicle of delivery. In both the Old Testament and the New Testament, prophecy was not primarily foretelling the future, but proclaiming the will of God and encouragement.

The adjudication of the gift of prophecy is twofold:

- The person giving the prophecy may speak in the normal language to the hearing of all.
- The person giving the prophecy may speak in tongues for another person to interpret the tongues in the normal language for all to understand and benefit from the ministration of prophecy.

> If any man speak in an unknown tongue, let it be by two, or at the most by three, and that by course; and let one interpret….and let the other judge.
> —1 Corinthians 14:27, 29

The ministry of the prophet

The ministry of the prophet is a level between the gift of prophecy and the office of the prophet. People serving in the ministry of the prophet are in most cases those who have operated in the gift of prophecy once and are now progressing into the next realm within the prophetic ladder. In this level, the word of wisdom, the word of knowledge, and the discerning of spirits manifest in their ministrations.

A person in the ministry of the prophet cannot claim to be a full-blown prophet in the clout of one in the office of the prophet notwithstanding the evidence of traits of word of wisdom, word of knowledge, and discerning of spirits in their ministration.

A typical scriptural example of people in the ministry of the prophet was the "sons of the prophets," students of the college of the prophets in Bethel and Jericho. They had prophetic insights into Elijah's rapture moment before he became the second human in church history after Enoch to be whisked away in the rapture in rehearsal:

> And the sons of the prophets that were at Jericho came to Elisha, and said unto him, Knowest thou that the Lord will take away thy master from thy head to day? And he answered, Yea, I know it; hold ye your peace.
> —2 Kings 2:5

Operating within the ministry of the prophet does not make one holder of the office of the prophet; otherwise, how would these sons of the prophets welcome Elisha after Elijah's rapture, and make obeisance to him as the replacement of Elijah who fits to be treated as the "national prophet"?

The underlying principle and ministry truth is that God does not raise dual or multiple holders of the office of the prophet in one geographical location. There could be several people in the office of the ministry of the prophet, but there is always only one exalted prophet with the clout for the office of the prophet amongst them. In operating the gift of the word of wisdom in the ministry of the prophet, the prophet in this region is graciously enabled with insight into certain futuristic occurrences.

Again the person with the ministry of the prophet gift is able to operate in the word of knowledge, which enables him or her to have knowledge of a past and present development. Furthermore, a prophet within the ministry of the prophet has reasonable discerning of spirits in order to complete the basic spiritual accouterment needed for a reasonably functional ministry of the prophet.

The office of the prophet

The office of the prophet and the office of the apostle are the two highest offices within the hierarchical structure of the church.

During the Old Testament era, the office of the prophet was an amalgam of all the fivefold ministries, but God in the New Testament dispensation, perhaps bringing more excellence into ministry, has broken it into five compartments. Nonetheless, this does not negate the importance of the office of the prophet in the New Testament setup.

It takes the acquisition or accumulation of certain qualities and experiences to be able to fulfill certain responsibilities, and this principle or factor is even more pronounced and indispensable to the holder of the office of the prophet. Seven tabulated points below feature preeminently in this regard:

1. Must be mature in the theology of the church.
2. Must be Biblicist.
3. Must have had longstanding relationship with God.
4. Must be one with operational experience in the gift of prophecy, word of wisdom, word of knowledge, and the discerning of spirits.
5. Must be one who flows in the supernatural, i.e., is one with the healing and the miracle gift.
6. Must be one who is able to lead and inspire.
7. Must be one whose words do not fall to the ground. This last quality, very rarely seen even among the veteran prophets, is one of the most convincing qualities of the holder of the office of the prophet.

And Samuel grew, and the LORD was with him, and did let none of his words fall to the ground.

—1 SAMUEL 3:19

The Prophet and the Seer

A seer in the literal sense is one who sees, but in a broader usage of the word from biblical perspective it means a prophet. Thus the word *seer* and the word *prophet* are used interchangeably toward one designation—the office of the prophet. This is effusively portrayed by Samuel, a doyen of a prophet who in this instance labels himself as a seer, in 1 Samuel 9:18–19:

> Then Saul drew near to Samuel in the gate, and said, Tell me, I pray thee, where the seer's house is. And Samuel answered Saul, and said, I am the seer: go up before me unto the high place; for ye shall eat with me today, and tomorrow I will let thee go, and will tell thee all that is in thine heart.

A worrying development emerging in the church today is the unrestrained proliferation of the prophetic ministry by pseudo-prophets, and others who see through the means of familiar and cultic spirits but parade the corridors of the church as prophets.

This is a prevailing global situation, but I must add that Africa and other geographical regions where idolatry was prevalent prior to the intrusion of Christianity are the areas in which this is most endemic.

It thus behooves the fivefold ministers and the church at large to place a high premium on the gift of the discerning of spirits if this "invasion" is to be halted.

The devil is a metamorphic, masterful tactician. He knows when to play the devil, and knows when to try to play God, as evidenced in Acts 16:16–18:

> And it came to pass, as we went to prayer, certain damsel possessed with a spirit of divination met us, which brought her masters much gain by soothsaying: The same followed Paul and us, and cried, saying, These men are the servants of the most high God, which shew unto us the way of salvation. And this did she many days. But Paul, being grieved, turned and said to the spirit, I command thee in the name of Jesus Christ to come out of her. And he came out the same hour.

Bill Alsop, stressing the inevitable intrusion into the church of the various forms of satanic practices, cautions the church to be high in the operation of the gifts of the discerning of spirits:

> There will be increased occurrences of new age philosophy as we approach the new millennium. It will be imperative for believers to operate in this

gift. We must be able to identify and deal with such things as occultism, witchcraft, black magic, and other satanic manifestations.[1]

Contrasting the Gift of Prophecy with the Word of Prophecy

The gift of prophecy is the standard gift that the Holy Spirit gives the prophet as mentioned in 1 Corinthians 12:10, and in the case of Ephesians 4:11 with respect to the ministry of the prophet and the office of the prophet:

> And he gave some, apostles; and some, prophets; and some, evangelists; and some, pastors and teachers.

Conversely, the word of prophecy is a special unction that the Holy Spirit attaches to the Scriptures to add value to the prophetic color of the preached or spoken word in order to bring enforcement to the promises of God inherent in it.

The operation and effectiveness of the word of prophecy is conditioned by the interaction, fellowship, and relationship of the person through whom the spoken Word, or preaching word, is released.

The efficacy of the power of the Word of God as annunciated in Hebrew 4:12 is contingent on the cordiality of the intercourse between the Giver of the promise (God) and the "giving" (the person has with God given out the promises of God to the listener, i.e., you). And in this instance, 1 Corinthians 3:9 comes into prominence:

> For we are labourers together with God: ye are God's husbandry, ye are God's building.

It becomes an issue of the more godly you aspire to become, the more godlike the spoken Word from your mouth becomes. When God takes over your life entirely, everything that you do carries with it the touch and seal of divinity.

In subliming the fivefold ministries, it will not be out of theological truth to state that people called into the fivefold ministry go into it with a very special unction of the word of prophecy to engender the reality of the Word of God reflective of Hebrews 4:12.

It must be stated unambiguously that when God does the calling into the fivefold ministry, the called must reciprocate by living within the virtues of ministry in order to access this exceptional impartation.

Everything God gives is conditional, and privileges, they say, entail responsibilities. You would not have any chickens to count if you ate the eggs.

The Prophet 79

GRAPH OF THE PROPHETIC DOMAIN

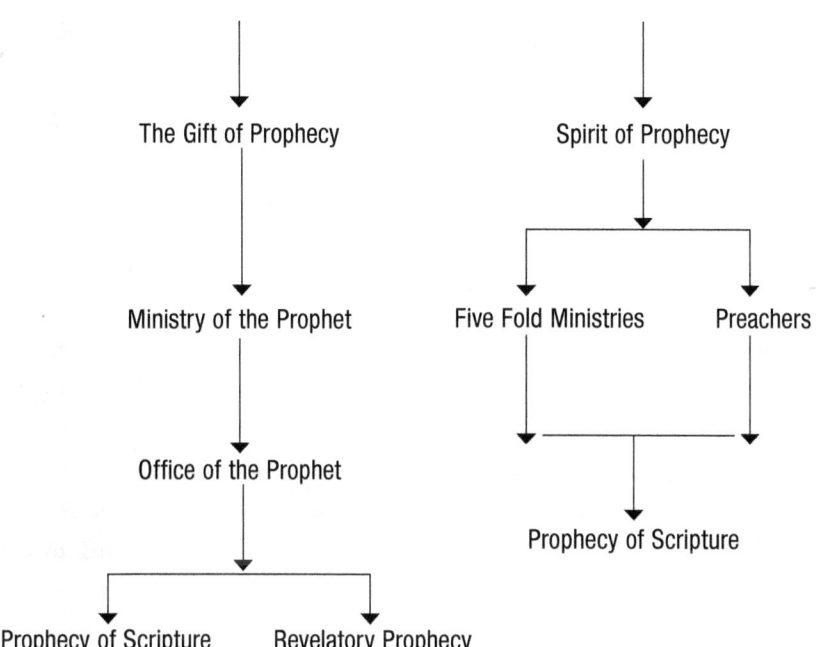

Chapter 11

THE EVANGELIST

The Branches of Ministry (Fivefold Ministry Gifts)

JESUS' PERSONALITY IS UNRIVALED in human history. He was the incarnation, God in the flesh, in the midst of humanity. In ministry, Jesus is the capstone.

In the prophetic domain, Jesus was prophecy in fulfillment. In apostleship, Jesus is the chief apostle. In evangelism it is said that never did a man speak like Him.

In the pastoral, Jesus had such compassion that after ministering to over ten thousand souls (with men numbering over five thousand), He had to miraculously provide bread and fish to feed them, with the surplus exceeding five baskets. He not only met their spiritual needs, but He also met their physical needs.

And in teaching, the message of the beatitudes in Matthew 5:1–12 stands out as the greatest expository teaching of all time.

THE PIVOTAL POSITION OF THE EVANGELIST

Jesus would be remembered more as a soul winner than for any segment in the other four ministries that could befit Him.

The ministry of the evangelist comes into prominence when taking on the fivefold ministries one by one. Evangelism was the pivot around which the ministry of Jesus revolved. In fulfilling prophecy, Jesus made sure that souls were won into the kingdom.

In the apostolic pursuit, Jesus made sure that nothing sidelined the soul-winning pursuit. In adjudicating the prominence of the office of the pastoral ministry, Jesus made sure that it came behind soul winning. And in teaching, the oracles of God were unfolded to send people into the kingdom of heaven, indicating the prominence of evangelism in the Messianic ministry.

The centrality of evangelism is seen from the perspective that it beclouded all the other ministries in the fivefold ministries during the Messianic era, which spanned about three and a half years. The Messianic admonition in Matthew 28:19, which is laden with evangelistic impulse and doubles as the benchmark for ministry, should be the preeminent focus of all the fivefold ministries:

> Go ye therefore, and teach all nations, baptizing them in the name of the Father, and of the Son, and of the Holy Ghost.

Even in the Old Testament era, the acuteness and necessity of the face and message of the evangelist were constant features in the prophetic enclave, as the affable prophet Isaiah indicates in 6:8:

> Also I heard the voice of the Lord, saying, Whom shall I send, and who will go for us? Then said I, Here am I; send me.

Who Is the Evangelist?

The evangelist could come under several descriptive captions, and the seven descriptions below generally fit the person being addressed:

1. One who prepares the way of the Lord as evidenced in the ministry of John the Baptist (John 1:23).
2. One eating with the zeal of the Lord to save the lost.
3. One with the eyes, the nose, the mouth, the ear, and the hand for the lost. From another angle, the evangelist could be described as the insatiable soul winner.
4. Generally one who is sent or goes to villages, towns, cities, and nations solely to proclaim the good news.
5. A minister without a parish or a congregation to preside over due to his frequent "gospel voyage." He is always on the move, so time does not permit him to stay longer at a given place for the norms of ministerial practices.
6. One with an unusual anointing and wisdom to convert sinners to Christ.
7. One with an insatiable hunger and thirst to convert the sinner to Christ.

The ministry of Philip the evangelist (Acts 21:8) gives a holistic picture of the work of the evangelist according to the New Testament pattern.

Philip preached the gospel of Christ, which was essentially the gospel of salvation and not the gospel of prosperity (Acts 8:4–5).

Many were saved and baptized in water (Acts 8:6, 12).

Signs, miracles, healings, and deliverance from evil spirits accompanied his preaching (Acts 8:6–7, 13).

He was concerned that the new converts be filled with the Holy Spirit (Acts 8:12–17).

Evangelism was the anchor head of the pursuit of the pioneer apostles, and as such, evangelism should be of prime importance in the programs and aspirations of the present church.

To this end the evangelist is essential to God's purpose for the church. The church that fails to encourage and support the ministry of the evangelist will cease to gain converts as God desires. It will become a static church void of growth and missionary outreach.

And most importantly, the church that values the spiritual gift of the evangelist and maintains an earnest and ongoing love and care for the lost will proclaim the message of salvation with convincing and saving power (Acts 2:14–41).

Of all that we do in ministry, it is only the platform of evangelism that offers us the greatest means of reward in heaven.

The apostle is needed to lead, the prophet is needed to guide and comfort, the pastor is needed to shepherd, and the teacher is needed to teach, but without the fruits of the evangelist all the offices of these ministries would have been rendered meaningless, or magnanimously put, partially inoperative.

Paul, seeing evangelism as the capstone in the fivefold ministries, especially with regards to the commensurate rewards associated with soul-winning ministries, says it philosophically here in Philippians 4:1:

> Therefore, my brethren dearly beloved and longed for, my joy and crown, so stand fast in the Lord, my dearly beloved.

Thus to the church, the office of the evangelist, and for that matter evangelism, becomes an imperative and not an option.

The Three Types of Evangelists

The evangelistic world is occupied by three types of evangelists: the Word evangelist, power evangelist, and revival evangelist.

The Word evangelist

Every evangelist is a preacher of the Word, but the Word evangelist's mainstay and cutting edge is the pinpointed preaching of the Word of God.

To the Word evangelist there is no other vehicle outside the preached Word to turn the unsaved into a convert. Consequently the Word evangelist is very well prepared and meticulous in the delivery of his or her evangelistic homily.

Four exceptional qualities mark the Word evangelist:

1. Organizational ingenuity
2. Extensive knowledge of homily topics
3. Homiletical prudence
4. Exquisiteness and clarity of delivery

Organizational ingenuity: Billy Graham, touted as the greatest evangelist of the twentieth century, is the epitome of a Word evangelist with rare organizational ingenuity. Billy Graham often spent months planning his crusades, and this reflected in the extensive and elaborate organization very well present in most of them. From the seating arrangements to the service of the ushers, and from the lighting arrangement to the platform orderliness is the power of planning and organization in retrospect.

For a non-miracle-working evangelist to attain the result that Billy Graham attained meant the man had unparalleled organizational qualities aside from his inch-perfect and down to the grassroots evangelistic homilies.

Extensive knowledge of homily topics: The Word evangelist does not stuff his crusade preaching with a lot of theological technicalities, loading his evangelistic sermons with a lot of theological words. The sermons of the Word evangelist are always simple, clear, and precise.

Unbelievers are different from the churched. To them Christ can never be known and seen if He is presented from an angle of theological sophistry. In this way the Word evangelist makes Christ happier by the way He is presented. As the King of kings, Christ was never born in an environment fit for the birth of a prince; instead, He was born in a manger.

Christ never lived to His billing as the Son of God in terms of flamboyance associated with the name, and Philippians 2:8 is a quintessential projection of this fact:

> And being found in fashion as a man, he humbled himself, and became obedient unto death, even the death of the cross.

In a nutshell Christ lived a simple lifestyle so He could be presented in a simple way for the simple man to be simply saved.

And Christ presented in a simple way is indicative that the presenter has an extensive knowledge of the God in the flesh who led an unusually simple life.

Homiletical prudence: Long and extensive preaching, no matter how good it might be, most often tends to lose its appeal. Homiletical prudence is delivering the homily within a sensible timeframe so the audience can appropriate and go home well with the message.

The above is a conspicuous quality of the Word evangelist. Like the master surgeon, the Word evangelist goes directly to the essential points of the sermon, cuts what should be cut, removes what should be removed, and gets the job done professionally, clinically, and quickly. The person who does not know Christ needs the short, pinpointed type of preaching, not the long, "let-me-doze-off" type of preaching.

Exquisiteness and clarity of delivery: The message of the Word evangelist is usually short, straight to the point, factual, and well emphasized.

These are all inherent ingredients of an exquisite sermon. And when these parameters are present in a sermon, its clarity is tangible.

The power evangelist

Power evangelism is the response to the Messianic promise to the early apostles and Christendom at large, as chronicled in Mark 16:17:

> And these signs shall follow them that believe; In my name shall they cast out devils; they shall speak with new tongues.

The church was established in the power of the Holy Spirit to replicate the power of God. The Trinity is strongly represented in these dualistic terminologies—ultimate in power and infinite in wisdom.

The Holy Spirit's coming strongly upon the hundred and twenty disciples on the Day of Pentecost during the commissioning and inauguration of the church therefore was in the direction of replicating the power and wisdom virtues of God.

God the Father is a power evangelist; that is why He related to the Israelites in power. And so awesome was His power that the Israelites asked Moses to tell God to spare them His personal interaction:

> And mount Sinai was altogether on a smoke because the LORD descended upon it in fire: and the smoke thereof ascended as the smoke of a furnace, and the whole mount quaked greatly.
>
> —Exodus 19:18

Jesus Christ, our Lord, the personal manifestation of God, was the Trinity's power evangelist. The description in Mark 7:37 is a summation of His power evangelistic prowess:

> And were beyond measure astonished, saying, He hath done all things well: he maketh both the deaf to hear, and the dumb to speak.

The Spirit God used humans instrumentally; the early disciples were His vehicle of power evangelism. The whole Book of Acts is tagged the ministry of the Holy Spirit, and today too, people who avail themselves of the Holy Spirit's presence are used as the vehicle of the ministry of the Holy Spirit.

Every life is activated by power and by seed. We see the power of the sun as it is involved in the growth of seeds, trees, and plants; and when asked what makes things grow, the undeniable answer is, the sun does.

By analogy, and in practical terms, the Holy Spirit is like the power of the sun; and He is God. The Trinity planned and programmed that the Spirit become the "anchorman" among them to bring the seed of the Trinity into man, activate the seed in tandem with the Word, and ultimately breathe life into all the Trinitarian ventures and interests on Earth.

Power evangelism takes a cue from the above. Three distinctive qualities and marks are associated with the power evangelist:

1. Explosive preaching
2. Ministration associated with intensive prayer
3. Signs-and-miracles related ministry

Explosive preaching: Men of faith are men of steely conviction, apologists who hammer home their faith in an explosive manner during their preaching.

Stephen was one of the leaders of the early church who was given such power and wisdom to preach the gospel in such a way that his opponents could not refute his biblical argument in defense of the sonship of Jesus to God, as well as His deity.

Stephen's explosive preaching was laden with oratorical power, miracles, and healing power, as explicitly stated in Acts 6:8:

> And Stephen, full of faith and power, did great wonders and miracles among the people.

Explosive preaching is better done by ministers who are filled with the Holy Spirit and the zeal of the Lord. The determination of these ambitious preachers, is to replicate Daniel 11:32:

> But the people that do know their God shall be strong, and do exploits.

Unfortunately, some Pentecostal and charismatic preachers today tend to use gimmickry and play to the gallery of the congregation. I have never been comfortable with such church room theatricalities, which I call the seeping of "Hollywoodism" into the church. That is what many of the congregants want; they want excitement, and some of these preachers make sure that they have their money's worth when they fill the pews.

In such a milieu, the sinner is comfortable in the pew, the believer equally at ease in the church chairs, and room is made for everyone who shows up in the church. But the pew is not supposed to be a comfortable friend of the straying believer, or the moribund Christian who is in incorrigible affinity with the world.

Looking at the positive side of this ministry, there are pockets of healing and deliverance that attest to the power of God.

Ministration associated with intensive prayer: This type of ministration is the stock of the trade of the evangelist whose ministry is characterized by a high dosage of prayer. At such meetings the speakers preach short messages before moving into ministration for the manifestations of the signs and wonders.

This prayer-filled domain of evangelistic ministry is the preserve of the practitioners of prayer. It you are not a very practically praying person you cannot be in a ministration associated with prayer, for you have to be involved in something before you can reasonably engage in it.

Signs-and-miracles related ministry: There is no better way to project the power or the hand of God than for signs and miracles to accompany the preached Word. And this is the ultimate for the power evangelist, to let people see, know, and experience God's power revealed through the gospel and carried aloft by the power preacher.

If it were not for signs and miracles, the gospel could not have gotten anywhere. Africa and other areas previously deeply involved in occultism have been won over chiefly by signs-and-miracles evangelists, whose gospel crusades attract crowds of hundreds of thousands, if not millions.

The development is a sequel to the events of the early church, when unimaginable power followed the preaching of the early apostles, as recounted in Acts 5:12:

> And by the hands of the apostles were many signs and wonders wrought among the people.

The revival evangelist

Revival is not a menu for the unbeliever; revival is a menu for the believer. Thus the unbeliever needs the power of the Word evangelist to restore his or her relationship with God, while those in the church whose relationship with God has nose-dived need the revival evangelist to straighten them up and quicken them toward an invigorating relationship with their Maker.

Revival in the Christian life is not a one-shot accomplishment, but it should be a periodic development; otherwise, why should the incomparable Paul in Philippians 3:10 speak relative to revival in his life?

> That I may know him, and the power of his resurrection, and the fellowship of his sufferings, being made conformable unto his death.

Prior to the incarnation, John the Baptist had to play the role of a revivalist to prepare the hearts of the people before the commencement of the ministry of Jesus Christ.

Biblical connoisseurs opine that the church began with a revival and the church age must end with a revival. If this is rightly so, then the need for the revival evangelist becomes even more acute.

Again, in this narcissistic age, and the era of extreme humanism, it would take only the fire from heaven to stem the tide of the "rotten apple" estate of this world. It is the revival evangelist who is best suited to stand in the gap and address the issue appropriately by the special anointing and grace that accompany the office.

Two types of revival evangelists are addressed: the Elijahic revivalist and the weeping revivalist.

The Elijahic revivalist: The Elijahic revivalist is the "fire come down from heaven" type of preacher. They brood no nonsense, and do not condone and connive with those who attempt to disdain God. They are extreme apologists.

The legendary prophet Elijah seems to be the progenitor of such preachers. Elijahic revivalists are fiery men and women of God who are always ready to take on society, or a nation, in defense of God. They are fearless and have such faith that they will do everything to see the name of God remain sacrosanct in the midst of heathenism, as amplified by the "fire calling" of Elijah in 1 Kings 18:38–39:

> Then the fire of the LORD fell, and consumed the burnt sacrifice, and the wood, and the stones, and the dust, and licked up the water that was in the trench. And when all the people saw it, they fell on their faces: and they said, The LORD, he is the God; the LORD, he is the God.

The weeping revivalist: Jeremiah was a weeping revivalist, and the best choice as reference for the weeping revivalist.

Unlike the Elijahic revivalist, who is an action man ready to call down the power of God upon recalcitrant sinners whose acts and deeds sorely provoke God, the weeping revivalist's stock of trade is speaking God's message and often lamenting to God.

The lamentations of the weeping revivalist do not always hinge on the individual sins of the people, but on a nation's general apostasy of godliness and the things of God, a situation very relative to the present sodomic lifestyle.

Today's ministry pattern and pace hardly give room for weeping. Too much ministry today is about self—how much I can do, how much I can accomplish, and how big a name I can make for myself. Consequently, self has sidelined God in ministry. Many ministers fail to recognize the bleeding heart and the weeping eyes of God, and are unable to articulate divine concern to the whole of humanity for redress.

When self rules and reigns, God is distanced; once God is distanced, He can never be heard; and if He is never heard, how can the church hear the progressive *rhema* God periodically has for His people?

Yes, God's authoritative Word for us comes from the *logos*, the written Word—but who says God does not frequently analyze situations and bring a specific *rhema* out of the *logos* to address concerns that arise out of noncompliance to the *logos*?

Indeed God has spoken (*logos*), but He continues to speak (*rhema*) in consonance with His identity as described in Hebrews 13:8:

> Jesus Christ the same yesterday, and today, and forever.

This Rapture generation is one that calls for more Elijahic and weeping revivalists to bring "order" to the present disorderly spiritual and societal terrain of ungodliness.

THE EVANGELIST

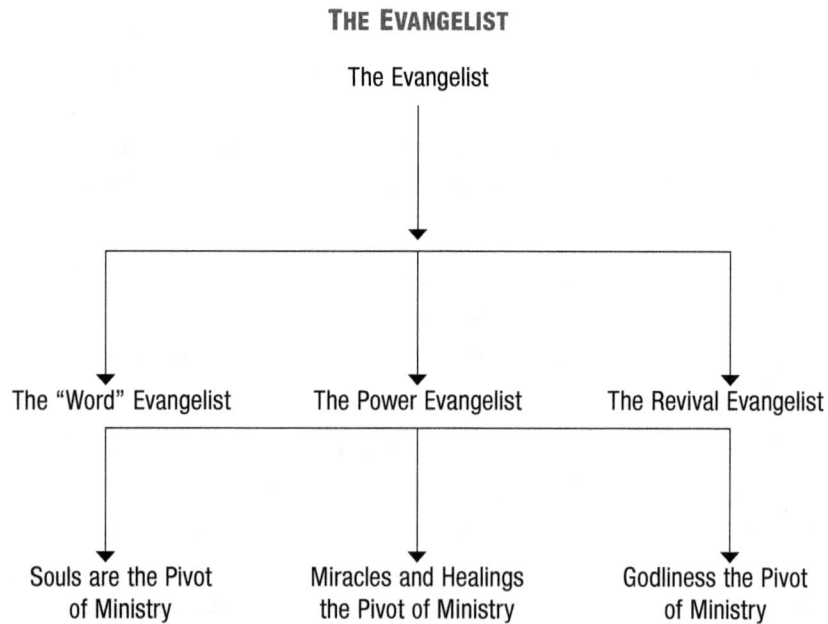

Chapter 12

THE PASTOR

The Branches of Ministry (Fivefold Ministry Gifts)

The person and ministry of the pastor is of utmost importance, especially within the setting of the church, as it is the pastor's job to groom and prepare the souls en route to the Rapture. Pastors are those who oversee and care for the spiritual needs of a local congregation. They are variously called elders (Acts 20:17; Titus 1:5), bishops, or overseers (1 Tim. 3:1; Titus 1:7).

TASK AND STRATEGIC PLACEMENT

The task of pastors is to proclaim sound doctrine, refute heresy (Titus 1:9–11), teach God's Word, exercise leadership in the local church (1 Thess. 5:12; 1 Tim. 3:1–5), be examples of purity and sound doctrine (Titus 2:7–8), and take care to see that all believers remain in the grace (Heb. 12:15). Acts 20:28–31 enjoins pastors to safeguard apostolic truth and the flock of God by being on the alert for false doctrine and false teachers who arise within the church. As the overseer, a pastor is to function as a shepherd, following the model of Jesus as the Good Shepherd .

The pastor is essential to God's purpose for His church. The church that fails to select a godly and faithful pastor will cease to be governed according to the mind of the Spirit (1 Tim. 1:13–14). It will be a church left open to the destructive forces of Satan and the world (Acts 20:28–31). The preaching of the Word will be distorted and the standards of the gospel lost (2 Tim. 1:13–14). Many will turn away from the truth and turn aside to fables (2 Tim. 4:4).

On the other hand, if a godly pastor is appointed, believers will be nourished by the words of faith and sound doctrine, and will be disciplined for the purpose of godliness (1 Tim. 4:6–7). The church will be taught to persevere in the teachings of Christ and the apostles, and thus ensure salvation for itself and those who hear (1 Tim. 4:16; 2 Tim. 2:2).

THE FOUR TYPES OF PASTORS

The personage and ministry of the pastorate can be broken into four compartments based on specialty and inclination:

1. Shepherd Pastor
2. Leader Pastor
3. Counseling Pastor
4. Family Pastor

These compartmentalized specialties do not take anything away from the all-embracing nature of the work of the pastoral ministry.

The shepherd pastor

The shepherd pastor assumes the spiritual responsibilities of a shepherd. The ministry inclination of this pastor is to shepherd and nurture his relationship with the "sheep," the congregation under his pastorate.

The duties of a shepherd in an unenclosed country like Palestine were very exacting. In early morning, the shepherd would lead the flock from the fold to the spot where it was to be pastured, marching at its head. Here, he meticulously watched them all day, taking care that none of the sheep strayed. If one of the sheep eluded his watch and wandered away from the rest, he sought it diligently until he found it and brought it back. John 10:11 bespeaks of the Good Shepherd, our Lord Jesus Christ, in relation to the above:

> I am the good shepherd: the good shepherd giveth his life for the sheep.

In those lands, sheep required to be supplied regularly with water, and the shepherd had to guide them to running streams or to wells dug in the wilderness and furnished with troughs. At night the shepherd would bring the flock home to the fold, counting them as they passed under the rod at the door to assure that none were missing. The shepherd's work entailed a reasonable measure of danger, from the attack of wild beasts to the wily attempts of the prowling thief through the dark hours.

In summation, the cutting edge of the shepherd pastor lies in their profound compassion and pervasive sensitivity to the plight of the sheep under his care.

The leader pastor

The leader pastor is the most liberal among the four pastoral identities. The leader pastor is a very contemporary person with regards to the perceptions and conceptions of life, and he loves to follow the tides of time.

Some of these leader pastors go beyond their line and end up being tagged "motivational speakers."

Most leader pastors frown on the idea that Christians should console themselves on the promise that we are going to walk on golden streets in heaven. To them, if gold will be our streets in heaven, then we need a ceaseless flow of dollars in our finances while here on Earth. And you cannot begrudge them if you have a telescopic view of Scripture within the perspective that the Christian life on Earth, which is a shadow of the reality of life in heaven, should give us an idea of what heaven will be.

The leader pastor is very practical and also adept at understanding the realities of the common man, specifically the ideals of those in the church who are not well grounded. This unveils his communication ingenuity—sharing common grounds with those who are not yet established in the church.

And in this direction, we reference the professorial tutelage of the contemporaneous Rick Warren:

> You can't communicate with people until you find something you have in common with them. The ground we have in common with unbelievers is not the Bible, but our common needs, hurts, and interests as human beings.[1]

The leader pastor, as a visionary, infects his audience with vision. If you sit under a man or woman who is filled to overflowing with the Holy Spirit, you become filled yourself. In the same vein, if you sit under or associate with a visionary, you become envisioned.

The life of substance, the life with substance, and the life of and with focus is lived around a vision. Without vision one may stroll through life in any way, with an unknown destination as the final port of berth. Conversely, a life that is lived by vision, upon vision, and with vision always has a person in control who knows where to land.

Today's great megachurches are pastored by leader pastors who are well informed and laden with vision to impart to the congregation. Men and women who fill the pews must ultimately appreciate the Bible and theology. If this were to materialize, the pastor would become the umpire between God and the congregation.

Whatever man lost in the Garden of Eden has been given back to us by God. The giving is the Lord's, but the receiving is our responsibility. And to be able to receive, biblical and theological knowledge and insight are essential.

But the capstones in this pursuit are leader pastors who bring their enormous spiritual, mental, and physical leadership to bear on the congregation.

The counseling pastor

Counseling is something that every pastor should be conversant with. However, there are some pastors whose strongest point in ministry is counseling.

The importance of counseling to ministry is not farfetched. Jesus Christ, the epitome of and our Chief Shepherd in ministry, carries a counseling accolade to buttress this fact, as described in Isaiah 9:6:

> For unto us a child is born, unto us a son is given: and the government shall be upon his shoulders: and his name shall be called Wonderful, Counsellor, The mighty God, The everlasting Father, The Prince of Peace.

Today's fast-paced life, coupled with unpredictable economic, environmental, and social factors, creates a counseling vacuum in society. The following points are some of the major factors necessitating the acute demand for counseling, specifically biblical counseling:

- There is a breakdown of personal morality, and no matter how hard the church and other stakeholders entreat society to return to the old ways of life, response seems to be at the lowest ebb.
- Along with the breakdown of the family, we are facing a sick society that is producing emotional problems at the pace that Japan produces automobiles.
- Humanistic answers to life's problems in this narcissistic age do not work, as only the manufacturer of an item is able to fix any associated problem of the product. God thus becomes the last resort, hence the acute need for the counseling pastor.
- The referral system is becoming a two-way street.
- More people are saying, "We've tried this and we've tried that, and nothing seems to work. Does the church have anything to say about this?"

Helping people overcome their problems through counseling can be one of the most satisfying arms of the pastoral ministry. But notwithstanding the satisfaction that comes from counseling ministry, it is the Achilles' heel of many pastors in geographical regions where demonism held sway before the intrusion of gospel power.

The devil is a master tactician who always adopts new and sophisticated strategies when his previous attempts failed. Therefore, counseling has become one of the most fertile grounds on which to knock God's servants "unconscious." For this reason, the Christian counselor must look out for these pitfalls:

1. A pastor must know when he is in "over his head," and to whom he can refer difficult cases.

2. Developing emotional attachment to the counselee should be a slipping sign for the pastor to back off the whole process and refer the counseling to another person.
3. If you do not have a husband or wife at home who has absolutely won your heart, refrain from a prolonged counseling session with a person of the opposite sex.
4. Feeling overwhelmed may be the first sign that the Christian leader should take a break, rest for awhile, refresh, and regroup.
5. Losing objectivity.
6. Gradual detachment from one's devotional life is the beginning of the flashing of the "yellow sign."
7. Beware of gifts from counselees.
8. Beware of unjustified eulogies from counselees.

The family pastor

The family pastor, as the name connotes, is a pastor whose cutting edge in ministry is on the solid-rock relationship he establishes with the sheep under his fold. To the family pastor, relationship with the sheep must be so profound that the sheep see him as being part of their families.

The family pastor exudes infectious love and compassion in his dealings with the sheep. As persons are not only the object of God's love but also the means through which the living Christ is made known, the family pastor fashions his ministry along the path of this biblical truth. Alvin Undgren's remark relative to the above is worthy of insertion here:

> The scriptures are clear that love for God is to be shown through love for persons.[2]

The church is God's temple on Earth. The church is the bride of God on Earth. The church is the ambassador of God on Earth. The church represents the image of God on Earth. And the church is the family of God on Earth, with an apt family name, "the household of faith," as revealed in Galatians 6:10:

> As we have therefore opportunity, let us do good unto all men, especially unto them who are of the household of faith.

The household of faith is the choice name for the church, God's bride, and His family on Earth. It is worth recalling that the family fact was the reason for the creation of man.

God's desire to have a human family culminated in the creation of Adam first and later Eve to facilitate this purpose. Without the family fact, it would be difficult to understand the reason for the redemption.

When Adam fell from grace to grass through his own volition to break the family ties with God, his Maker, it created a huge gulf in the heart of his Maker. That gulf could not be filled by angels, though they are a very compliant creation.

Consequently the Son God had to come to die and reconcile fallen man to God, all towards the restoration of the family fact.

Every person loves the family, especially when the family band is intractably woven around love, compassion, care, and affection for each other. There is nothing more beautiful than a family honed in and knit together in love, by love, and for love.

The family factor brings God's people together and helps to shape a common identity for the family. Thus the ministry of the family pastor goes a long way in fusing his godly nature, characteristics, and concepts into the families that he ministers to.

Godly personality is formed through our relationship with God, and persons who have a closer relationship with God. Conversely, relationship is deformed through personal relationship of a negative nature

From this perspective, the person and ministry of the family pastor is one of strategic importance to the shaping and identification of the constituents of the household of faith with God.

The church must be a haven for fellowship of redemptive love, and to this end the pastor, specifically the family pastor, holds the key to actualizing this ideal. The pastor is the role model and the pacesetter in every godly pursuit in the church. Therefore, once he sets the tone, the sheep follow admirably.

Church administration is primarily about people, and everything about people operates by the dynamics of love and relationship. And since everything about love and relationship is instructive, the acme of the pastoral ministry is at the level of family ties, where the family pastor is seen as the knitting point, intruding into families with the love of God and with his own warmth of heart.

The Dynamics of Conflict Resolution in the Pastoral Ministry

Ministry is about people and for the betterment of people. It is here that conflict resolution comes into play as one of the focal areas of the work of the pastor.

The pastor then becomes the therapist, the counselor, the guide and the "Mr. Fix-It." Fix what? Fix broken relationship among siblings. Fix what? Fix broken limbs in marital relationships. And fix what? Fix divine/human relationship.

But the fixation would only be a mirage if the right parameters were not put in place to create a conducive atmosphere . To build you must create the favorable foundation beforehand, and to fix you must first create the enabling conducive human and personal relationship.

People are more open to those with whom they have already established some measure of personal relationship. You cannot trust a person you barely know. You can only trust, to some extent, a person you have already established some relationship with. Thus the family pastor is essentially important in the administration of the church vis á vis the dynamics of conflict resolution.

Conflicts have become unavoidable, the "unwanted beasts" in human institutions. The pastoral ministry therefore must be adequately resourced to present a formidable front against the "beast" of conflict that is desecrating homes, schools and institutions.

The Two Faces in the Pastoral Ministry

There are two faces in the pastoral ministry. These are 1) the full-time pastor and 2) the bivocational pastor.

The full-time pastor

The full-time pastor is the pastor who is fully employed in the church, working the full day, and fully supported and salaried by the church. These pastors are overseers in congregations that have enough human and financial resources to make full-time work possible.

Pastors who work full time in big churches do not work alone. Some of the fortunate full-time pastors have associate pastors and other staff members to augment the administrative responsibilities placed under their jurisdiction.

If the church is big and the leaders humane, cooperative, and supportive, the office of the pastor becomes a paradise on Earth. However, if one does not find a very cooperative and humane leadership to work with, under such a milieu the work tends to be very frustrating, and unenviable.

The bivocational pastor

The bivocational pastors, to me, are the heroes in the ministry. You may not understand my frank assessment if you have never functioned in this capacity before.

These are people who work hard at their various workplaces and still manage to squeeze in time to respond to the hard realities of the pastoral ministry.

Without the bivocational ministers the work of God would have stalled in many nations, especially in the developing ones. The iconic Paul states the position of the bivocational pastor in 2 Corinthians 12:14:

> Behold, the third time I am ready to come to you; and I will not be burdensome to you: for I seek not yours but you: for the children ought not to lay up for the parents, but the parents for the children.

A Graph of the Pastoral Ministry with Jesus as the Chief Shepherd

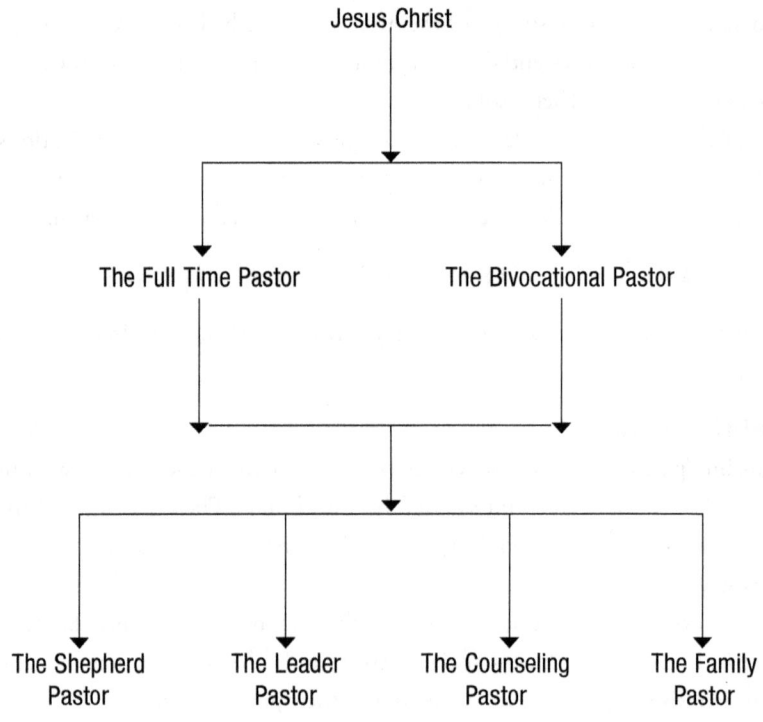

Chapter 13

THE TEACHER

The Branches of Ministry (The Fivefold Ministry Gifts)

THE OMNISCIENT AND OMNIPOTENT Trinity, in giving the fivefold ministry gifts to the church, composed the ministry in a manner as to bring about checks and balances to its operation.

God is the all-powerful God, and He also is the all-wise, and all-knowing God. When God acts in power, He guides it by His wisdom. That is why He does not need to review His acts once He presses the button of delivery.

In giving the gifts to humanity for the work of the ministry, and also to replicate His acts, some people were gifted with the power gifts whilst others received the wisdom gifts. The purpose of giving the wisdom gifts was to curtail any excesses that might arise out of power.

It was in pursuance of the above objectives that the teaching ministry was incorporated in the fivefold ministry gifts.

Though teaching is the last to be mentioned in the fivefold ministry gifts, its placement does not necessarily mean that it ranks least in importance with regards to the fortunes of the church.

To God, all the ministers in the fivefold ministries command equal importance and therefore these gifts were given to reflect their overall importance to the church and as a manifestation of the profound depth of divine wisdom:

> Wherefore he saith, When he ascended up on high, he led captivity captive, and gave gifts unto men. And he gave some, apostles; and some, prophets; and some, evangelists; and some, pastors and teachers.
> —EPHESIANS 4:8, 11

For a holistic delivery of the divine purpose, God supplemented the fivefold ministry functions with the "body gifts" (which shall be addressed in the subsequent chapter) with the intention of ensuring a well-lubricated engine for optimum ministry delivery.

Etymology of the Word

To "Grecize" a little, *didaskalos* is the Grecian rendition of the word *teacher*, and it generally refers to a doctor, master, or teacher.

And in the Hebraic form the words *Rabbi and Rabboni* emerge relative to the doctor, master, or teacher.

Rabbi

Rabbi ("my master") is a title of dignity given by the Jews to their doctors of the law and their distinguished teachers. It is sometimes applied to Christ (Matt. 23:7, Mark 9:5). That the Jews treated their teachers with utmost reverence is undoubted. This perhaps accounts to the abuses of reverence associated to this title by the Pharisees, who ultimately became aristocratic in the Jewish society, all in the "holy placement" of the teacher.

Rabboni

This word occurs only twice in the New Testament ("Lord," Mark 10:5; "Rabboni," John 20:16). John 20:16 refers to the reverence and sublimity that was attached to its usage:

> Jesus saith unto her, Mary. She turned herself, and saith unto him, Rabboni; which is to say, Master.

The Who and the Functions of the Teacher

Teachers are those who have a special, God-given gift to clarify, expand, and proclaim God's Word in order to build up the body of Christ (Eph. 4:12).

Teachers may be described as the lawyers of the Bible, with the primary task of safeguarding and defending the "constitution" of the church, which is the Bible.

It becomes imperative, therefore, for the teacher to be abreast with all the fundamental issues of the Scriptures if they are to fulfill the primary purpose of their placement.

It would thus not be out of place to demand that the teacher ought to be a "Bible worm" in order to be able to rise up to the dynamics of the teaching ministry, as Paul's admonition to Timothy indicates:

> Study to shew thyself approved unto God, a workman that needeth not to be ashamed, rightly dividing the word of truth.
>
> —2 Timothy 2:15

- The special task of teachers is to guard, with the help of the Holy Spirit, the gospel entrusted to them (2 Tim. 1:11–14). They are to faithfully point the church to biblical revelation and to the original message of Christ and the apostles, and to defend the truth with steely determination at all times. Thus apologetics within the fivefold ministry essentially reside in the teaching ministry.

- The principal purpose of biblical teaching is to preserve and produce holiness by leading the body of Christ into an uncompromising commitment to the godly style set forth in God's Word. Christianity is a practical vocation, and the practicality of our Christianity must manifest in the love, purity, faith, and sincere godliness we portray to the outside world. Thus what we learn must not only remain within our mental faculty but must be exemplified through the life that we live in the flesh.

- Teachers are essential to God's purpose for His church. When the church refuses to hear the teachers and the theologians they are endowed with, it is rejecting the people the Holy Spirit has placed in the church to preserve the genuineness of the biblical message and correctly interpret the original teachings of Christ and the apostles.

The faithful teachers and theologians are the doctrinal "troubleshooters" of the church. Once they are operative in the church, spirits of heresy and schisms hardly find fertile ground in which to operate.

Without the teachers and the theologians, new winds of doctrine would be uncritically accepted and religious experience and human ideas, rather than revealed truth, would become the ultimate guide to doctrine, standards, and practices of the church.

Without the teachers and theologians, the organism seed and spirit which originate from God would systematically be detached from the church; and in this development the church would be turned into a haven of human organization where human philosophies and ideas dictate the business proceedings.

The charismatic gifts and their operations, and the other apparatuses of the church need constant supervision and scrutiny, if you like, and without the teachers whose "eagle eyes" always bring the needed checks and balances into church, the spiritual symmetry of the church would be eroded. Thus the beauty and excellence of God, vis á vis the charismatic gifts, is better safeguarded by the carriers and couriers of the spiritual gifts.

Without the teacher there would be extremism in the adjudication of the spiritual gifts. First Corinthians 14:29 is reflective of the supervisory mandate given to the teachers and leaders of the church in this respect:

Let the prophets speak two or three, and let the other judge.

The Qualities of a Teacher

- The teacher must have some "painting qualities." This does not mean literally possessing painting abilities, but the ability to turn the Scriptures into readable and observable objects for a better understanding and assimilation of the intent and content of the message

- The teacher must emphasize harmony in teaching, and have the ability to blend ideas and biblical truth into a compact unit.

- The teacher must be an exponent of biblical truth. Biblical truth of impacting proportions must ooze from his or her teachings.

- The teacher must be a reasonable biblical academic who has reasonable truth to share and teach when called upon, or as is demanded of his ministry. These enjoin the teacher to be a good student of the Bible himself.

- The teacher must be a person of patience. Every good teacher has a tolerable, broad and accommodating heart to be able to receive all shades of opinions and questions for address.

- The ability of discernment is a major prerequisite for the teaching ministry. Any teacher without this essential quality could be beaten by the spirits of deception, heresy, etc., which the devil constantly plants in churches to champion his diabolical intentions.

- The teacher must not be excessively critical. They must have the "culture of the benefit of the doubt." Jumping to conclusions and never giving the other party the opportunity of expression or explanation is "unteaching."

The Conservative and the Liberal Teacher

Society is an evolving entity, which is why there is an element of dynamism about everything of man, with man, and about man. It is therefore imperative that the teaching ministry become a dynamic ministry in order for it to not be outpaced by the fast-paced cultural evolution we are going through, which ultimately affects every fiber of societal life.

The tag—the conservative teacher and the liberal teacher emerge from the spillover of the cultural change that society goes through, which is a reflection of the two broad-based ideas, thoughts, and philosophies that influence societal persuasions at any given point in time.

The conservative teacher

Conservatism has its roots in the thoughts, ideals, deeds, and practices of the founding fathers.

The conservative teacher is the teacher whose beliefs and doctrinal inclinations are tailor-measured to those of the progenitor, or progenitors, that he came to meet. Or magnanimously put, the conservative teacher is the teacher whose beliefs and teachings are mostly derived from his mentor, or the originator of what he mostly believes and practices.

The problems that Jesus Christ encountered in ministry arose primarily from the quarters of the conservative teachers of the day who were intractably glued to the then sacrosanct Mosaic doctrine and teachings which were diametrically opposed to the emerging teachings of grace advocated by our Lord and Savior. Jesus did not altogether reject everything from the Mosaic stock; His problem with the Pharisaic teachers of the law at the time stemmed from their deviation from the Mosaic law into teachings that were strictly human and traditional. Jesus Christ, alluding to the hypocrisy and sycophancy of the Pharisaic teachings, cautions His disciples:

> For I say unto you, That except your righteousness shall exceed the righteousness of the scribes and Pharisees, ye shall in no case enter into the kingdom of heaven.
>
> —MATTHEW 5:20

Conservative teaching, doctrine, and belief do not reside only in the Old Testament segment of the Bible. Even within the contemporary New Testament setting we find both conservative and liberal beliefs.

Jesus was an advocate of both the conservative and the liberal teachings. What He was against was tradition and humanism. Jesus did not overthrow or overturn the law; instead He spoke for its maintenance along with the addition of the doctrine of grace, which made the channels of divine and human relationship holistic.

Grace, without doubt, is the factor that restores the broken relationship between God and man. But after the restoration it takes the works and fruits of grace, of which the law forms an essential component, to ensure the sustenance of the gracious grace imputed to us as a result of the blood of our Lord Jesus Christ.

Salvation by grace does not negate the need for compliance to the law; in fact it enforces the demand for compliance:

> What shall we say then? Shall we continue in sin, that grace may abound?
> —ROMANS 6:1

The liberal teacher

Teaching is dynamic, and the dynamism of teaching is in consonance with the dynamics of society. Society operates within the principles of progression; therefore, as society progresses and becomes more dynamic, so does everything within follow the evolving trend in society. It is in this respect that liberal teaching emerges to flow with the unfolding trends in society.

The liberal teacher is the teacher who adapts her thinking to suit the taste of contemporaneous trends. From another perspective, the liberal teacher could be described as the teacher who molds her teaching principles and practices to toe the line of the taste of the present generation.

This does not mean that the liberal teacher wholeheartedly sidesteps the teaching foundations that he came to meet. What it means for the liberal teacher to adapt to the present circumstances is that he refines, rephrases, and repackages the original content in line with the modern scope of understanding to make the content and intent of the original clearer and more easily digestible to the contemporary citizenry.

Liberalism in its quintessence is adding value to conservatism without diminishing the conservative outlook and perspective. It does this by holding on to the conservative ideals albeit repackaging to suit contemporary taste.

Jesus Christ was both a conservative and a liberal teacher. He taught the fundamental Word but infused it with the power and authority reflective in liberalism, as depicted in the officers' reply to the Pharisaic authorities who sent them to arrest Jesus:

> Then came the officers to the chief priests and Pharisees; and they said unto them, Why have ye not brought him? The officers answered, Never man spake like this man.
> —JOHN 7:45–46

A holistic appraisal of liberalism incorporates the latter biblical translations. Modern-day translations of the Bible arose out of the desire of the Bible scholars to keep pace with modern thinking and ideals reflective in liberalism.

To the liberal Bible scholars, the King James Version appeared too colloquial in vocabulary. Therefore, the need for a Bible couched in modern language to meet modern and contemporary needs, which are integral elements of liberalism, necessitated the dozens of modern-day translations of the Bibles on the shelves.

Through the many modern-language editions of the Bible on shelves, the dynamism of liberalism is in vogue.

The King James Version of the Bible was produced out of a desire to get a language of the Bible cognizance with trends at that time. At that time, during the era of King James, that edition of the Bible named after that legendary English king was the standard, and the contemporary edition of the Bible.

Today, the New International Version and other contemporary editions have taken over. And tomorrow, newer editions shall come in print to reflect liberal ideals.

And what about the liberal advertisement that claims if King James were alive today, he'd be reading the New International Version?

A Graph of the Fivefold Ministry

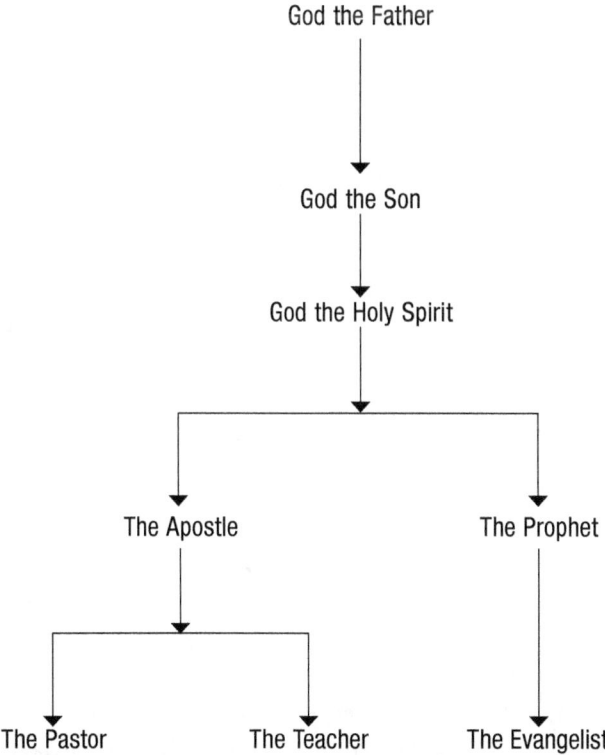

Chapter 14

THE "BODY GIFTS"

THE HUMAN BODY IS composed of two major parts: the head and the body. And relative to the charismatic gifts or the gifts of the Holy Spirit, the Spirit's impartation is administered to reflect the head gifts and the body gifts.

The "head gifts" of the body of Christ are those enumerated in Ephesians 4:11, whilst the "body" gifts of the church are those enumerated in 1 Corinthians 12:7–10.

The "body gifts, " just like the head gifts, are given by the Holy Spirit optionally, not by the imposition of anybody's wish and will on the Holy Spirit:

> But all these worketh that one and the selfsame Spirit, dividing to every man severally as he will.
> —1 CORINTHIANS 12:11

Before we set out to enumerate the body gifts, it is imperative to bring about this dichotomy between the head gifts of Ephesians 4:8–11, and the body gifts of 1 Corinthians 12:8, relative to the time span or duration of the gifts in the life of the recipient.

By their sublime placement, the ministry gifts, which essentially are leadership gifts, have an element of calling attached to them, bringing into their innate being some measure of permanence.

The fivefold ministries are offices of calling, and when God calls He does not repudiate the calling, a view amplified in Romans 11:29:

> For the gifts and calling of God are without repentance.

Another point of clarification is that it is unscriptural and unwise to assume that because someone has exercised a spectacular gift, that person is more spiritual than one who has less spectacular gifts.

Christian maturity, and for that matter spiritual maturity, is not in the enclave of the administration of the charismatic gifts. For instance, someone can come to church today and become fortunately and graciously gifted with any of the body gifts in 1 Corinthians 12.

Now does that mean that this "baby" Christian, though gifted, could instantly become more mature than the person who has been in the church for years and is exuding fluidly the fruit of the Spirit, which is the benchmark in the determination of Christian maturity?

Furthermore possessing a gift does not mean that God approves of all that a person does or teaches. The spiritual gifts are totally different from the fruit of the Spirit that relates more directly to Christian character and sanctification as enunciated in Galatians 5:22-23:

> But the fruit of the Spirit is love, joy, peace, longsuffering, gentleness, goodness, faith, Meekness, temperance: against such there is no law.

A Christian's overdependence on the charismatic gifts to the neglect and desuetude of the characteristic gifts which manifest the fruit of the Spirit could be detrimental to the growth and destiny of the individual, and the church at large.

THE LIST OF THE BODY GIFTS IN 1 CORINTHIANS

The apostle Paul lists a variety of body gifts that the Holy Spirit gives to believers, and these are mentioned and briefly exegeted here, as they have come under a more profound treatment in an earlier chapter.

The gifts could be put into three compartments, and therefore they shall be mentioned and treated in this order. The word of wisdom, word of knowledge, and discerning of spirits are my first picks, based on the fact that they form the "eyes of God" in the church, and judging by the strategic function of the eye to the body generally.

Word of wisdom

Word of wisdom is divinity's gracious impartation unto us to savor a little of the infiniteness of God.

Our God, who is the ultimate in power and infinite in wisdom through word of wisdom, gives us this unique opportunity to glean in the future what is about to happen in the life of a person for whom this gift begins to unravel.

In defining word of wisdom, Bill Alsop's snappy explanation would fit in very well here:

> Word of Wisdom is supernatural insight into God's divine purposes and will.[1]

Word of wisdom is a wise utterance spoken through the operation of the Holy Spirit, relative to the needs of somebody.

On the other hand, having the wisdom of God for daily living does not come as a charismatic gift but through diligent study and meditation on God's ways and Word, and by prayer (James 1:5–6).

Within the fraternity of the body gifts, word of wisdom emerges as its "binocular."

Word of knowledge

If the Spirit of God reveals concerning the future, then He reveals concerning the past as well. The same Spirit God that gives the Word of wisdom also gives the Word of knowledge:

> To another the word of knowledge through the same spirit.
> —1 Corinthians 12:8

The word of knowledge, which has some measure of connectivity to prophecy, is an utterance inspired by the Holy Spirit that reveals knowledge about people, circumstances, or biblical truth.

The operation of word of knowledge usually has to do with events past and present. The gifts of the Spirit, though different in their entity, have a catalytic element in their operation; the operation of one gift often leads to the performance of another gift, which completes the process that was started by the first gift.

A typical example of this feature was the Old Testament scenario between Elisha and the Assyrian army. Elisha's word of knowledge operation exposed the military strategy of the Assyrian army, and it climaxed when the entire army was blinded relative to the miracle gift (2 Kings 6:8–23).

By virtue of its ability to recollect events past and present and bring them to the notice of the church and individuals, the Word of Knowledge could be described as the "historian" of the body gifts.

Discerning of spirits

Discernment and discerning of spirits have often been considered one item. Though identical by outlook, there are dissimilarities in their operations and functionalities.

The element of commonality about discernment and the discerning of spirits is that both involve perception; this is perhaps attributable to the marriage of the two by some people.

Discernment may not always involve the spirit world, in that one may have discernment based on intellectual knowledge and experience.

On the other hand, discerning of spirits is a supernatural manifestation of the Holy

Spirit. Because it is a prime gift of the Holy Spirit, everything about it is a manifestation of the Holy Spirit. By definition, discerning of spirits is a supernatural gift given to a believer, giving him or her the ability to distinguish or perceive what is influencing a person or situation.

In sieving the power of influence behind a person or situation the discerner of spirits is able to distinguish whether the spirits are:

- Demonic
- Flesh activated
- Angelic
- Spirit inspired

In a world fraught with deception, subtlety, inconsistencies, and other "Luciferic" virtues, the discerning of spirits becomes the one gift that the church needs most. In the inaugural era of the church, discerning of spirits was very conspicuous and broad-based in the ministry of the apostles. It was this gift that exposed and subsequently led to the punishment of Ananias and his wife Sapphira in Acts 5:

> And Ananias hearing these words fell down, and gave up the ghost: and great fear came on all them that heard these things (v. 5).

The devil used subtlety and deception to dislodge our first parents from the Garden of Eden, and in these final moments of the lease period of the earth, he is very much at the acme of his chiefest weapon, deceiving people and turning them into his surrogates to endure eternal suffering with him.

Discerning of spirits is one gift that its importance cuts across board. The fivefold minister acutely needs it and so does every person in the church. Whether in ministry or not, each Christian has a common enemy who is an expert in deception.

The only gift that is able to detect him before he draws closer to hatch his diabolical plans is the discerning of spirits, hence the need for every member of the household of faith to possess this particular gift.

Towards the end of the age, when false teachers and the new age philosophy are on the loose, the gift of the discerning of spirits will become extremely important to the church.

Faith

Great men and women whose exploits have left behind indelible imprints were people of faith. Smith Wigglesworth's name comes to mind as one of the contemporary exponents of faith; no wonder he was referred to as "The Apostle of Faith," as a quote in his book depicts:

> Smith Wigglesworth was called "The Apostle of Faith" because absolute trust in God was a constant theme of both his life and his messages.[2]

The gift of faith is among the gifts that constitute the "hand" of God in the charismatic gifts fraternity.

Faith is the fuel that drives all the charismatic gifts. The gifts of the Holy Spirit are not operated in an ambience of timidity and fear. God is a forceful God, and therefore any attributes given to humanity for service are laden with force. Two factors that become indispensable to the operator of the gifts are faith in God, and faith in oneself. Faith in God puts the feet of the operator of the gifts firmly in the omnipotence of God. By this the gifted puts her absolute trust in God to be able to safeguard her in the operation of the given gift.

Faith in oneself is the ability to believe that one is in God, and the operation of God in him or her; therefore every step taken to effect the operation of the gift does not have an iota of incapability on his or her part.

Experientially, when the gift of prophecy started to operate in my life, the initial problem I had was pessimism as to whether I was moving by the Spirit of God, the spirit of man, or the spirit of the devil, anytime I had the inspiration of the spirit of prophecy. I had to gather faith before I could be used of the Spirit in this ministry. And when I finally settled in my "stride" by acquaintance with the operation of the gift through faith, pessimism gave way to fluidity of operation.

Three types of faith emerge from the faith stable: 1) Saving Faith, 2) Developmental Faith, and 3) Supernatural Faith.

Saving faith

Our salvation comes as a gift of God's grace; but it can only be appropriated by the human collaboration, and response of faith. So then, saving faith could be appropriately described as gracious faith that God gives sinners to see themselves as sinners, and see Jesus Christ as their Savior.

Salvation comes by the grace of God. And the response to appropriate the salvation which comes by faith can never be engineered by the sinner. It is a gracious faith that the Holy Spirit activates in the spirit of the sinner before appropriating the salvation of grace.

So God gives salvation by grace and then activates the faith in the heart of the sinner, which becomes gracious faith to complete the process. Romans 3:23–24 gives us the biblical authentication:

For all have sinned, and come short of the glory of God; Being justified freely by his grace through the redemption that is in Christ Jesus.

Developmental faith

Developmental Faith connotes the faith that one develops after receipt of the inaugural faith of grace that ushered one into salvation, and into Christianity.

Developmental faith seems to suggest that God does not continually spoon-feed His children. He expects us to show some measure of responsibility after the weaning processes in the "new birth" are over.

Thus He gives you the faith of grace to be saved, and subsequently expects you to develop your own faith through His Word and your interaction with His Spirit in order to be able to stand on your feet.

Through God's grace that enables us to have the requisite faith for salvation, and from there to developmental faith, we are enabled to have a taste of who and what God is experientially.

From there our experience of God adds weight to our Christian conviction, and as Christianity becomes experiential it thus leads to evidential, which subsequently gives the agnostic theory no footing in the Christian's life.

And under such a milieu, the synergistic power of the charismatic gifts and the characteristic virtues of the fruit of the Spirit work in tandem for a common purpose—the solidity of the faith and conviction of the Christian.

There are three broad outlets of developmental faith:

1. Faith involves repentance. Once we are born again we gradually have to turn from all acts, relationships, and companies that are at variance with the Word of God and Christian practices. This development does not, however, come with a bang. It comes gradually as we interact with mature Christians and frequent the house of God. Repentance is a willingness to turn from evil and seek God and godliness:

   > Now when they heard this, they were pricked in their heart, and said unto Peter and to the rest of the apostles, Men and brethren, what shall we do?
   >
   > —Acts 2:37

2. Obedience to Jesus Christ and His Word is a major ingredient of faith. One cannot live in disobedience to the Word of God and have faith in the same Word. It does not work and it cannot work. Obedience to the Word becomes a major foundation of faith,

especially within the perspective of developmental faith. In determining our love for Jesus Christ, obedience to His Word becomes the major benchmark. You cannot claim to love God when you are living in absolute disobedience to His Word:

> If ye love me, keep my commandments
> —John 14:15

In developmental faith, in which cometh obedience, the principle of "your master is the one who you obey" is invoked.

3. Faith has a master, and one's master is whom he or she is attached to. Thus faith includes a heartfelt personal devotion and attachment to Jesus Christ. This expresses itself as trust, love, gratitude, and loyalty toward Him. Faith and love are bedmates; if you have faith in someone you certainly would love that person, and this is why Jesus admonishes in Matthew 22:37:

> Jesus said unto him, Thou shalt love the Lord thy God with all thy heart, and with all thy soul, and with all thy mind.

Supernatural faith

Supernatural faith is faith beyond saving faith, and beyond developmental faith. It is faith beyond our natural faith.

The gift of faith is a supernatural manifestation of the Holy Spirit that elevates the believer to a realm of faith beyond the measure that has been proportioned. The supernatural faith elevates one's faith beyond his existing faith in order to carry out an assignment in line with divine purpose.

The gift of faith can also be the catalyst for other gifts, but it is essentially acute to the other power gifts—miracles and healing.

The power gifts represent the hand of God, which epitomizes His power and strength. As such the three power gifts exude an unusual anointing, or shall I call it back-up anointing, to be able to assert the power and strength of God during ministration.

When the gift of faith is in operation it strives for what others see as impossible. It is one gift that makes nonsense of all the form guide. Jesus' ministry was all-around supernatural faith, hence the disciples were so spellbound by this enigmatic figure that they were lost of words for him:

> And they feared exceedingly, and said one to another, What manner of man is this, that even the wind and the sea obey him?
> —Mark 4:41

When I traveled from Ghana to the States to go to college at Christ for the Nations in Dallas, Texas, I did it on the ticket of supernatural faith. The ticket for the journey was acquired through faith; somebody came to me saying the Lord had spoken to him to bring me the money. I left Ghana without anything in my pocket to cover my tuition, and yet I graduated and walked out of CFNI with a clean bill.

When I stepped on the plane en route to the States people termed my trip a risky undertaking, but supernatural faith turned it into a rosy undertaking. That is what supernatural faith does. It sweeps across everything that stands in the way of its fulfillment.

Great men and women of God were people great in faith, and specifically supernatural faith. They were people who were spiritual bulldozers; for when one is gifted with the gift of faith he becomes a bulldozer who clears everything on his way to ministry.

It is imperative to state here that people who are gifted with supernatural faith are men and women very strong in the Word. Their strength is in the Word, and through it they daily lubricate their faith armada. Supernatural faith people take the Word of God at the gross value and propel it at the gross value.

PROPHECY

If God has an eye and a hand within the body gifts, then He certainly has a mouth. Thus prophecy, various kinds of tongues, and interpretation of tongues which are facilitated through the human mouth aptly fit to be called the "mouth" of God.

Prophecy is the ability to speak an inspired utterance in the known language of the speaker and the hearer. This is prophecy within the body gifts enumerated in 1 Corinthians 12:10:

> To another the working of miracles; to another prophecy.

Prophecy under addressal here must be distinguished from prophecy under the ministry gift of the church in Ephesians 4:11. As a spiritual manifestation, prophecy is potentially available to every Spirit-filled Christian (Acts 2:17–18); and as a ministry gift, prophecy is given only to some mature believers, who must then function as prophets within the church. Acts 21:10–11 gives a picturesque insight of the latter:

> And as we tarried there many days, there came down from Judaea a certain prophet, named Agabus. And when he was come unto us, he took Paul's girdle, and bound his own hands and feet, and said, Thus saith the Holy Ghost, So shall the Jews at Jerusalem bind the man who owneth this girdle, and shall deliver him into the hands of the Gentiles.

The message of prophecy in the body gifts is three pronged: edification, exhortation, and comfort:

> But he that prophesieth speaketh to men to edification, and prophesieth exhortation, and to comfort.
> —1 Corinthians 14:3

Edification
To build up, causing spiritual growth and development.

Exhortation
To admonish; to appeal to one's character or conduct.

Comfort
To console, soothe, or speak in a tender, intimate way to someone.

Divers Kinds of Tongues

The inauguration of the church in Acts chapter two was done in mystery and in power. Cloven tongues as of fire, signifying power, sat on the disciples; and the disciples were mysteriously enabled to speak the languages of the many people from divers linguistic backgrounds who had assembled in Jerusalem to celebrate Pentecost, the second greatest feast of the Jews.

And Acts 2:6–9 gives us an overview of this dramatic spiritual unfolding:

> Now when this was noised abroad, the multitude came together, and were confounded, because that every man heard them speak in his own language. And they were all amazed and marveled, saying one to another, Behold, are not all these which speak Galilaeans? And how hear we every man in our own tongue, wherein we were born? Parthians, and Medes, and Elamites, and the dwellers in Mesopotamia, and in Judaea, and Cappadocia, in Pontus, and Asia.

In summation, the gift of divers kinds of tongues is the spiritual enablement to speak in a language one has never spoken before.

I think it will be fitting to close the thesis on the divers kinds of tongues by recapping the genesis of the many languages in the world today that did not exist in the early part of creation.

It all began with man craving fame. He wanted to get to God through human effort and ingenuity without God's approval, as captured in Genesis 11:4–5.

God's disapproval of that venture did not come from man's effort to build a skyscraper, but from the motive behind it—attempting to reach God through human effort for the purpose of pride: And they said, Go to, let us build us a city and a tower, whose top may reach unto heaven; and let us make us a name, lest we be scattered abroad upon the face of the whole earth (v. 4).

Linking Acts Chapter two to the Tower of Babel experience, the former was born out of the opportunity to see the power of God and to give honor to Him (Acts 2:7), and the latter by God to show man his limitation and the futility of the purpose of and the drive for pride.

The underlying lesson here is that self, ego, and pride hardly receive divine endorsement. The gifts are given so that in their administration God shall be glorified; the gifts are not given that the administrator shall build a castle of pride that extends to God.

INTERPRETATION OF TONGUE

Prophecy comes to the church through two means—direct prophecy and the interpretation of prophecy; and it is relative to the latter that interpretation of tongues becomes pertinent to our present study.

By definition, interpretation of tongues is the process where the interpreter, though he or she may not understand the language of the speaker, is able to give an inspired declaration of what was said in that language.

This does not mean that the interpreter would also have to be gifted in prophecy. He or she receives the inspiration to be able to interpret it perfectly to the understanding and assimilation of the gathering.

Thus it could be described that the interpreter of tongues is the bilingual secretary who ensures that the coded messages from heaven through tongues are decoded for the understanding and benefit of the church.

Chapter 15

THE IMPACT AND INFLUENCE OF ORGANIZATION

THE OVERARCHING IMPACT OF organization could be partially gleaned from this hypothesis: vision begets purpose, purpose begets organization, organization begets fulfillment, and fulfillment begets satisfaction or contentment. In this hypothesis, organization is the middle step, indicating its strategic placement in the life of any entity.

Kwame Nkrumah, a graduate of Pennsylvania University and the first president of Ghana, as well as Africa's man of the last century, is remembered most for his favorite cliche: "organization settles everything." His receiving the title of Africa's man of the last century was a feat achieved partly through his organizational ingenuity.

In theological circles, George Whitefield and John Wesley were reputed to be the most influential preachers of the eighteenth century. Although they were contemporaries and both were greatly used by God, today George Whitefield's name is in the archives of history, but John Wesley's name is both in the archives of history and on the lips of people.

Between the two, Whitefield seemed to have more charismatic clout. But John, by his organizational acumen, created an organizational structure to fulfill his vision culminating in the birth of the Methodist Church, the second largest Protestant denomination today.

America is the most developed country in the world, and also ranks among the most organized countries in the world.

In contemporary American political history, Barack Obama was able to raise more money for his presidential campaign than any American presidential aspirant, largely due to his organizational ingenuity. It did not end there; he also was able to draw a historic crowd to the ballot box en route to his presidency.

If these indices would not tag organization as a strategic partner in fulfillment, I wonder what would.

The Roots of Organization

Organization takes its roots from God. Every act of God bespeaks organization. Humanity therefore cannot live contrary to the demand, ethics, and standards of organization.

We were created in the image and likeness of God; therefore we must live in consonance with the image and likeness of God.

The Father God is the pioneer organizer. When He decided to create, He did not just create for creating's sake; He did it based on organization. That is why there is so much order in creation.

When a person is organized there is so much orderliness in their acts; and acts that were planned with organization hardly go to the drawing board again for review. These acts become standard bearers that stand the test of time. Creation is the handiwork of excellence, and also the epitome of organization, to the credit of the Father God.

The Messianic Ministry was organization at its best. Jesus our Savior knew when to pray, when to preach, when to teach and when to do the miraculous. And the onlookers, after being stupefied by His ministerial organizational exquisiteness and performances, were drowned in the ocean of amazement:

> And were beyond measure astonished, saying, He hath done all things well: he maketh both the deaf to hear, and the dumb to speak
> —Mark 7:37

And it is a postulation of the indispensability of organization that the Spirit God established the church on the shoulders of the fivefold ministry.

Thus the offices of the apostles, the prophets, the evangelist, the pastor, and teacher in the fivefold ministry were given to ensure proper coordination and well-oiled organization:

> And he gave some, apostles; and some prophets; and some evangelists; and some pastors and teachers.

The Trinitarian paradigm behooves us to toe the line of organizational exquisiteness in our pursuits, first for our own appreciation, and second to replicate an essential virtue of God to reinforce our status as beings created in the image of God who are duly reliving their image billing.

The Definition of Organization

There are a myriad of definitions of organization, but these three from this research stable come for placement:

1. Organization means doing things properly and fittingly towards maximum results through organized structures. Every organized person works around structures, and when one works around structures there is coordination and cohesion in her pursuit toward maximum results which properly and fittingly dovetail into her overall aspirations. God created around organized structures. For instance, He created heaven before the earth (Gen. 1:1). He knew that the heavens would sustain the earth and therefore needed to be created first. That was organization in action.

2. Our esteemed and acclaimed efforts are depictions of the fruits of organization. That which is highly esteemed and acclaimed does not come to humanity like manna fell in the wilderness to the Jews, but from effort crafted around organization. Thus esteemed and acclaimed products are churned out by people with impeccable organizational abilities.

3. Organization is the influential son of wisdom manifesting prudence in his acts. This definition is akin to the biblical maxim that faith without works is dead:

> Even so faith, if it hath not works, is dead, being alone.
> —James 2:17

And talking about wisdom, King Solomon's name obviously becomes the pick in the "Good Book."

Solomon's wisdom manifested chiefly in the comprehensiveness of his organizational ingenuity that reflected in all strata of his life, culminated in people from all walks of life trooping to Jerusalem to catch a glimpse of arguably the wisest person to have walked on the earth:

> The queen of the south shall rise up in the judgment with this generation, and shall condemn it: for she came from the uttermost parts of the earth to hear the wisdom of Solomon; and, behold, a greater than Solomon is here.
> —Matthew 12:42

The Three Requirements of Organization for Success

Success does not come to us by chance, and generally success does not come to us through someone's sweat and toil. Although someone may help you at times over the course of life's journey, success essentially comes through your own output; someone cannot succeed for another person.

There are requirements to succeed, and these three demands of organization come into prominence:

1. Organize Your Life (Life Management)
2. Organize Your Vision (Vision Management)
3. Organize Your Time (Time Management)

Organize Your Life

Life has no substitute, and so therefore life must be lived preciously. Living your life preciously is in essence living an organized life; or simply put, organizing your life.

There are basically two qualities that take a person to the "roof of the building," the acme of one's purpose: charisma and character. Charisma (gift) is divinely released, and character (organization) is human-developed or activated.

To get to the highest in every discipline, one needs the charisma and the character. These two must be intractably woven in a person's life to ensure this—ultimacy in a pursuit perhaps reserved for "the gods."

Samson, in this wise, is our obvious pick for reference. Samson was, mildly put, prodigiously gifted. Indeed Samson was one of the very few people in the Bible gifted with strength. But Samson was enormously deficient in character; plainly stated, Samson did not have character. And because having no character means having no organization in one's life, Samson made a heavy weather of the purpose God had for him.

If you do not have character or organization, you will live in rebellion against the norms of life, the values of tradition, and even the prevailing common sense of your generation.

In all of the stated, Samson was awful. First, Samson rebelled against parental counsel and married the woman he was craving. Second, Samson broke his Nazarene oath by going in for a woman from an uncircumcised people. And third, when he as a judge was expected to be seeking divine counsel to be able to judge Israel, he was lost in sensualities, "waltzing" between the thighs of a woman.

For his refusal to organize his life, Samson broke the heart of a nation, broke the heart of God, and blew his own life:

> And Samson said, Let me die with the Philistines. And he bowed himself with all his might; and the house fell upon the lords, and upon all the

people that were therein. So the dead which he slew at his death were more than they which he slew in his life.

—Judges 16:30

Samson's charisma failed him because he did not realize that relying absolutely on charisma in ministry is so thin a line to walk on. Charisma is easier to acquire than character, and everything that is acquired easily cracks and ultimately caves in when subjected to extreme pressure.

In ministry, character is the foundation, hidden underneath which is the mainstay of the projected superstructure which is hereto referred as "charisma."

Organize your Vision

When God gives you a vision and an assignment, He does not go on from there to organize for you en route to fulfillment. At most He gives you the requisite wisdom which, when applied, hastens the actualization of the vision.

Churches that thrive are the churches with vision, especially those whose vision is well spelled out to attract the human resources and the money needed to push the vision to its elastic limit. Rick Warren's incisive advice is catalytic:

> The second thing to realize when thinking about church finances is that people give to vision, not to need. If need motivated people to give, every church would have plenty of money.[1]

God gave Joshua the vision and charge to lead the Israelites to the Promised Land. Joshua reacted promptly, and organized for action; the following verse is indicative of his swift, organization-laden response:

> Then Joshua commanded the officers of the people, saying, Pass through the host, and command the people, saying, Prepare you victuals; for within three days ye shall pass over this Jordan, to go in to possess the land, which the Lord your God giveth you to possess it.
>
> Joshua 1:10–11

How to Organize Your Vision

1. 1. First, recognize the vision you have. (You cannot organize what does not exist, or what you do not have.)
2. Plan the execution of the vision.
3. Prioritize the primary, secondary, and other phases of the vision.
4. Pace and pause in the execution of the vision.

5. Evaluate achievements within the planned phases of the vision.
6. Restrategize and rejuvenate if you are falling behind the plan or period of execution.
7. Seek cooperation and collaboration if need be.

How to Organize Your Life

1. Know yourself and who you are in the Lord (see John 1:12).
2. Recognize the gifts and talents in yourself.
3. Know where you have the comparative advantage.
4. Know what you are pursuing in life.
5. Plan, prioritize, pursue.
6. Develop a disciplined mind, a disciplined body, and a strong willpower.

Organize your time

Every being that operates by time believes in time management. Organizing your time means believing and practicing time management.

God believes in time management because He became time's maiden practitioner and gave it to guide us in fulfillment. The importance of time is seen within the perspective that everything that has a life span is regulated by time.

It is only God who is not subject to time because He is an infinite Spirit, and also the cause of time. He caused time to regulate His creation, not Himself.

Today's fast-paced life has made time a precious commodity. We hurry to work, we hurry to board the plane, we hurry to meet the departing schedules of trains and buses.

Even the foods we cook have time periods of cooking. Time seems to be controlling humanity today. In this respect, time management has become essential to the pursuits of our aspiration in life, and the normal requirements of societal life.

In this perspective we must live our lives by making our time count, not counting time. A disorganized life makes counting time pertinent, but an organized life makes time counting an integral part of one's aspiration and pursuits.

God is an astute believer and practicer of time management; otherwise how could He have created in six days in order to rest on the seventh day?:

> And on the seventh day God ended his work which he had made; and he rested on the seventh day from all his work which he had made.
> —Genesis 2:2

In our pursuit of time management, one salient fact ought to be the driving force in our approach: time was made for man, and not man for time. In this perspective, we do not allow time to rule and manage us; we rule and manage time.

From this angle we organize our life, vision, and time around our personage, and not our personage around the life we live, the vision we intend to actualize and the time available to us.

When you are organized, you live by the framework of your vision, plan, pursuits and fulfillments within the allotted time span. Living within time is indicative of the fact that you are organizing your time, and also organizing your life.

There is one indispensable principle associated with time: you either organize your time, or time will disorganize you.

Pitfalls to Time Management

Eight points offer a comprehensive addressal to the above, and they are tabulated below and given brief exegesis:

Procrastination

Procrastination is said to be the thief of time. Desuetude is a robber and a waster; it is a robber of purpose and a waster of vision, which cumulatively lead to unfulfillment.

What ought to be done should be done today, not put off for tomorrow. Today has its own work schedule and tomorrow will have its own workload.

Pilling up assignments brings excessive pressure on the body, which ultimately brings about stress. Put off the day's assignment only when you realize that exhaustion is stepping in after you have given the day your best shot.

After the death of Moses and in the course of the Exodus, God's anger started "boiling up" when He realized that the Israelites were procrastinating and had spent unnecessary time at the bank of the river Jordan, as recounted in Joshua 1:2:

> Moses my servant is dead; now therefore arise, go over this Jordan, thou, and all this people, unto the land which I do give to them, even to the children of Israel.

In His disappointment for their excessive stay on the bank of the Jordan, God instructed Joshua to not let "this Jordan" stand their way and ruin their time management.

Poor personal planning and scheduling

Poor personal planning and scheduling entail living the day by whatever comes into the mind and the heart. People of foresight are those rich in personal planning. When you plan and schedule well, you proceed smoothly and positively.

Interruption by people without appointment

This factor ought to be looked at critically, especially when the workload increases at the office.

People must be met and attended to by the manager's plan and schedule for each day, but not those who interrupt by walking in without the recourse of an appointment. Interruption by people who walk in without appointment is a management bane and a silent killer of executives.

Poor delegation

Delegation offloads some of the responsibilities of the manager to the delegated. In church management, the offices of the fivefold ministry are a quintessence of Trinitarian delegation.

Those in the fivefold ministry—the apostles, the prophets, the evangelists, the pastors, and the teachers—have the delegated power and authority of the Trinity to function on their behalf in the church, and to the world:

> And he (Jesus through the Spirit) gave some, apostles; and some, prophets; and some evangelists; and some pastors and teachers.

Delegation, when done with clear-cut designations, ensures rapid progression of the entity.

Poor use of the telephone

The telephone has a dualistic impact; one for positive result, and the other for negative result. In this wise, the telephone is a good messenger and at the same time a bad master.

As a good messenger, the telephone used judiciously could enhance any establishment. Conversely, any executive who will attend to the phone every minute certainly is not going to have enough time available to perform the essential official responsibilities.

In this wise, the telephonist becomes essential within the structure of the office, to act as a "troubleshooter" against unnecessary calls that would erode the performance of the manager.

Reading junk mail

If something wastes, it cannot be godly. God does not waste in any facet of His acts and deeds. When Jesus fed the five thousand, He ensured that the leftovers were not put in the trash. He asked the disciples to gather them into baskets (see Matthew 14:20).

The minister should distinguish between the "priority mail" and the "ordinary mail." The priority mail is the mail that could make relevant contributions to the day's schedule, and the ordinary mail is that which other people within the leadership could read and attend thereto.

Lack of concern for good time management

There is time management, and there is good time management. Time management is the norm, but the irony is, it gives some spaces for little leakages.

However, good time management goes further to ensure an "eagle eye" in the daily executive duties of the organization. It makes more sense to exercise good time management and have a longer holiday than to allow time to slip through your fingers and rob you of a longer vacation.

Every good executive is a time saver with a performance model that does not give room from intrusion; and this could only materialize through good time management.

Lack of clear priorities

Having priorities in management is good, but having priorities in perspicuity is the best in time management. In management you must have "head priorities," "body priorities," and "foot priorities."

The Effects of Organization Relative to the Mosaic Experience

Moses was a spiritual bulldozer, and an incomparable one as such. But when it comes to management, especially time management, he was grossly deficient. Perhaps Jethro, Moses' father-in-law, was a gift from God to address the managerial shortfall that would have ended his life abruptly.

The following ten points of time management principles are deduced from the Mosaic experience as chronicled in Exodus 18:16–23:

An organized person does the right thing in consonance with time management and priority of issues (v. 17):

> And Moses' father in law said unto him, the thing that thou doest is not good.

What Moses was doing prior to Jethro's timely intervention was, mildly put, foolishness. But Jethro was mindful of Moses' position—which had been elevated by God to post-presidential status and deserved something more than diplomacy—hence his retort to Moses, "the thing that thou doest is not good" (which is the diplomatic substitution for "the thing that thou doest is foolish").

An organized person is healthy (v. 18a):

> Thou wilt surely wear away.

Moses would have become a beast of burden of his own creation, which would have overworked his nerve en route to paralysis.

Jethro's timely arrival into the camp of the Israelites did a world of good to Moses and to the entire Jewish nation, which needed Moses more than ever at that crucial period. Due to Jethro's counsel, a better-organized Moses became a more relaxed and a healthier Moses.

People around organized persons or society are healthier than people around disorganized persons and society (v. 18b):

> Both thou, and this people that is with thee: for this thing is too heavy for thee.

Character traits and qualities affect and infect. Moses' disorganization prior to his re-orientation would have undoubtedly had a concomitant effect on the whole Jewish structure and people. Moses would have worn away, and the people would have been worse off.

Get an organized leader and you have an organized group, an organized community, an organized society and an organized country. And if the organized leader is one whose influence is pervasive enough to cut across nations and continents, then the whole world will be better off due to the organizational ingenuity of that solitary figure.

Organized people or leaders do not carry heavy loads alone (v. 18c)

Leadership is about responsibilities. Responsibilities are either shared with people around the leader, or carried by the leader alone. Moses had chosen the latter option as the sole carrier of the leadership responsibilities of the judiciary until Jethro got onto the scene with his timely counsel of delegation of responsibilities

Organized leaders normally concern themselves with policy formulation and leave the job to the technocrats on the ground (v. 19)

Jethro, in counseling Moses on the right thing to do, also crafted the details of his organizational innovation for a holistic result, as the verse under addressal projects:

> Hearken now unto my voice, I will give thee counsel, and God shall be with thee: Be thou for the people to God-ward, that thou mayest bring the causes unto God.

In every sound organization that exercises prudent time management and enjoys maximum results, the reason behind the soundness is clear cut and well spelled-out policy that enables the operations to produce to their maximum potential.

Jethro's counsel here addressed that concern. He tasked Moses to be a policy formulator by communing with God and spelling out the details for the leaders and the whole nation to follow.

Organized leaders believe more in training human resources and upgrading their competence for better performance (v. 20)

Jesus' leadership methodology was to teach, commission, and evaluate His disciples as a way of ensuring their competence for the job in His absence.

That is the hallmark of quality leadership; train the operators for the job. A leader should be able to train a colony of leaders so that he or she becomes the leader amongst the leaders.

Organization provides the directional tool for the personnel on the ground to do the work efficiently and effectively (v. 21)

Under such a milieu the responsibilities are entrusted to the leaders proportionally according to each leader's capability and competence, with all fronts headed for maximum output.

Proper organization ensures that the leadership concern themselves with only the top echelon jobs (v. 22)

In most organized organizations it is the rank and file who do the most demanding and manual work. Under such circumstances it becomes an issue of the leaders working with the heads, and the rank and file working with the hands and every part of their bodies.

Organized people are able to conserve energy for the requisite endurance for their lifelong fulfillments (v. 23a)

The right organization ensures that leaders do not dissipate energy that could be vital in the latter part of their lives:

> If thou shalt do this thing, and God command thee so, then thou shalt be able to endure, and all this people shall also go to their place in peace.

People under organized leadership do not live lives of restlessness, they live lives of peace and relaxation (v. 23b)

When you are organized, you are in firm control of your life; you know what you want to do, and when to do it.

People that live peaceful and relaxed life do not live this life by chance; they live it by their created structures on the ground that hone their activities into an organized unit to make that possible.

A BASIC STRUCTURE OF ORGANIZATION RELATIVE TO TIME MANAGEMENT

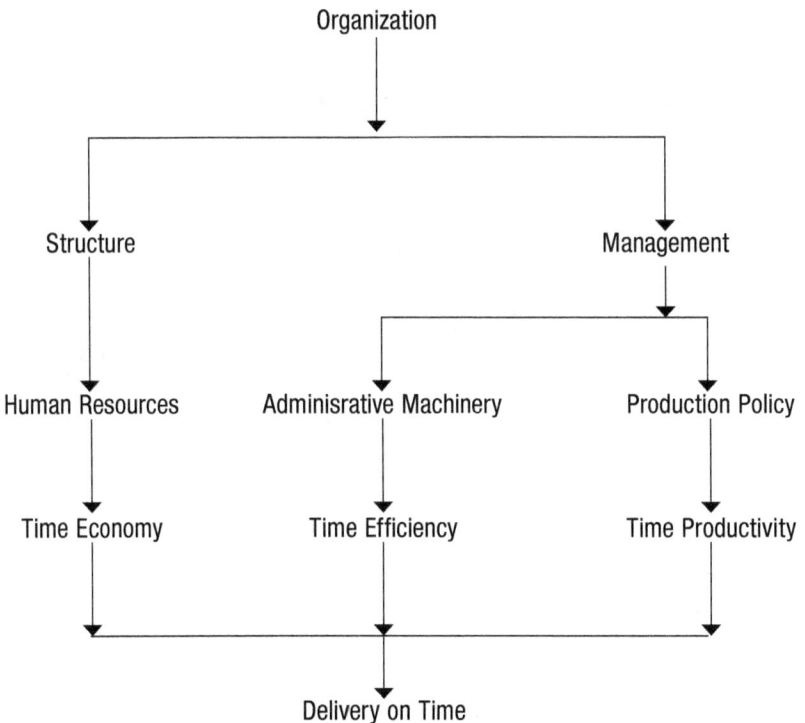

Chapter 16

LEADERSHIP

IT IS OFTEN SAID that leadership is something fit only for "the gods." This standpoint renders leadership unattainable and beyond the purview of human involvement; something that is the preserve of the gods should never be ventured into by humanity.

The basic understanding that comes from the above statement (which is clouded in philosophy) is that leadership is something of the highest responsibility that requires qualities that are supra human.

Leadership is a very complex term, placement, and position. It can make and it can unmake. Leadership is paradoxical, there is an attachment of sublimation to it, and there is a tag of humiliation on it; no wonder Leroy Eims, long-time director of evangelism worldwide for the Navigators, snappily cautions threaders of leadership:

> Before a person takes on a leadership responsibility, he should weight the matter carefully.[1]

DEFINITION OF A LEADER

Several definitions could be given to leadership viewed from the broad-based nature of the theme, and our attempt at fostering a definition of it would be sourced from a biblical perspective.

Three definitions thus come to mind with regards to who a leader is:

1. A leader is someone who leads.
2. A leader is someone into whose hands responsibilities have been entrusted.
3. A leader is someone called by God and anointed by God for a specific function.

A Leader Is Someone Who Leads

To lead means to have some people behind you counting on you to take them to a certain destination in life. This dimension of leadership is broad-based, with its tentacles covering the spiritual, physical, and mental worlds.

Defining the leader as someone who leads in its holistic presentation makes everybody a leader. The life that the Creator has graciously entrusted into our hands requires leadership—leadership from within and from without.

Leadership from within refers to assuming leadership over one's life, sailing one's "personal boat" to safe berth of accomplishing and fulfilling God's divine purpose for his or her life.

In life, great achievers become great leaders. And great achievers are able to brace the storms of the vicissitudes, the unpredictables, and the challenges of life that are inevitable to every person.

Generally what separates the achiever from the nonachiever is the ability of the achiever to take charge and lead in the journey of his life.

Humanity innately is a leader, and as is demanded of every leader, one is mandated to take charge and lead his or her life. In life, you either take charge and head towards your destined and crafted path, or someone else will take charge and mislead you towards the path to the unknown.

Further, any person who does not assume leadership of some sort over his life is invariably subjecting it to circumstantial control, which has the destination of "only God knows."

The following extract from a profound Pauline statement is indicative of one leading his life:

> Not as though I had already attained, either were already perfect: but I follow after, if that I may apprehend that for which also I am apprehended of Christ Jesus.
>
> —Philippians 3:12

Taking charge over circumstantial control in one's life reminds us of the Messiah's commanding the ravaging Sea of Galilee to calm down.

The Sea of Galilee measures about seven miles wide and thirteen miles long. It is seven hundred feet below sea level with mountains that rise three to four thousand feet, and frequently experiences unusually violent storms. And in one of such unfriendly weathers, the disciples were caught in utter fright as the imminent capsize of boat loomed.

Unable to take charge of the circumstances, they went to the snoring Jesus at the yonder part of the boat and awakened Him from His sleep. He took charge, rebuked and stilled the storm to teach the principle of circumstantial control. And the disciples commented in sheer admiration:

> And they feared exceedingly, and said one to another, What manner of man is this, that even the wind and the sea obey him?
>
> —MARK 4:41

A Leader Is Someone into Whose Hands Responsibilities Have Been Entrusted

The privilege of life is associated with the demand to be responsible, in conformity with the adage: privileges entail responsibilities.

This particular domain of leadership is akin to the entrepreneurial manager, and those who preside over the governorship of state apparatuses. Greater responsibilities are in the hands of such people, but unfortunately they often subject their offices to abuses of unethical and immoral proportions. Political and governmental leaders are worst off in this regard.

But casting the net wider for a broader purview of this definition, everybody's hands are entrusted with some sort of responsibility. And to catch everybody in this net by zeroing in on family relationships, the parents have responsibilities to the children, and the children have responsibilities to the parents.

A parent who shirks his parental responsibilities ceases to be a parent, and a child who does not treat her parents with honor ceases to be a child. The status is not the deal; the deal is within the responsibilities.

A Leader Is Someone Called and Anointed by God for a Specific Task

This type of leader is a spiritual leader. In addition to the spiritual leader, there is also the leader who, though not called, has been anointed by God for governmental purposes. In this regard, King Saul comes to mind:

> Then Samuel took a vial of oil, and poured it upon his head, and kissed him, and said, Is it not because the LORD hath anointed thee to be captain over his inheritance?
>
> —1 SAMUEL 10:1

Of the three definitions, the last is the one with strong divine attachment. The divine attachment to this rung of leadership manifests by way of the anointing.

The anointing is a process by which God empowers an individual to lead and perform feats that cannot usually be performed through normal human means and abilities.

David killed a bear, a lion, and a giant not because of his brute strength, but because of the anointing that was upon his life (see 1 Samuel 17:34–35). Samson did his exploits of brute strength through the Spirit that moved him, which in essence was the anointing that was upon his life:

> And the Spirit of the LORD began to move him at times in the camp of Dan between Zorah and Eshtaol.
> —JUDGES 13:25

THE THREE IDENTITIES OF LEADERSHIP

Leadership is descriptive, and everything descriptive has some element of form to merit description. In this direction, three identities of leadership emerge: 1) Leadership is an Art, 2) Leadership is a Science, and 3) Leadership is Empowerment.

Leadership is an art

The arts take their source from creativity, and if everything artistic is dynamic, then leadership, which is an art, is dynamic. Consequently, leadership, which is a describable art, comes with its descriptive color—style.

In summation to this identity, leadership as an art tends to project the leadership styles of a leader.

Leadership as an art goes along with diverse and varied styles. For instance, one leader could be a "team player," and his style of leadership could be to work the various strata and human resources of the organization into a compact unit where hierarchical details do not factor much into the operations of the sector.

Another style within the "team player" stable could be harmonizing the various strata and human resources for the organization but with some measure of recourse to hierarchy. That is style, and that is what brings leadership under the arts academy.

Even in the adjudication of the spiritual gifts, the Holy Spirit had to minister in a way relevant to multifacetedness of leadership styles as stated in 1 Corinthians 12:4–6:

> Now there are diversities of gifts, but the same Spirit. And there are differences of administrations, but the same Lord. And there are diversities of operations, but it is the same God which worketh all in all.

Leadership is a science

Leadership as science refers to the technicalities inherent in leadership. In this vein the principles that deal with the privileges, laws, and responsibilities of leadership emerge.

The domain of principles is so pervasive. It covers every facet of life—personal, institutional, and vocational.

It is a common fact that proven scientific laws are not alterable. So it is with leadership principles, which, though alterable, never leave the flouter free without dancing to the ramifications of his or her defiance.

Consider the ramifications when Miriam flouted the principles of leadership by accusing Moses of arrogating to himself too much authority and influence, as recorded in Numbers 12:9–10:

> And the anger of the LORD was kindled against them; and he departed. And the cloud departed from off the tabernacle; and, behold, Miriam became leprous, white as snow: and Aaron looked upon Miriam, and, behold, she was leprous.

The experience of Miriam gives us insight into the fact that whosoever flouts leadership principles never appreciates.

Leadership is empowerment

Empowerment is the receipt of extra force from above; leadership means receiving extra power and ability to be able to function as a leader.

Leadership as empowerment is essentially a spiritual development, though in the physical realm certain offices that are acquired through the process of voting qualify to be offices of empowerment. But since empowerment is poignantly in the spiritual, we place it under the spiritual echelon of leadership.

The Bible is replete with empowerment for leadership. Before Saul was enthroned as the first king of the Jews, the prophet Samuel had to be sent by God to anoint him to receive empowerment for the taxing demands of that high office arising out of the rebellion of the Jews:

> Then Samuel took a vial of oil, and poured it upon his head, and kissed him, and said, Is it not because the LORD hath anointed thee to be captain over his inheritance?
>
> —1 SAMUEL 10:1

Then David, arguably Israel's greatest and most adored king, was also anointed by the same prophet, Samuel, when God rejected Saul for breaching leadership law by arrogating to himself the office of the prophet, going ahead with the sacrifice instead of waiting for Samuel.

Saul forgot that the principle of division of labor within spiritual leadership is not negotiable (see 1 Samuel 13:9–14).

David's anointing as recapped in 1 Samuel 16:13 was associated with the visible impartation of the Spirit of God upon his life:

> Then Samuel took the horn of oil, and anointed him in the midst of his brethren: and the Spirit of the LORD came upon David from that day forward. So Samuel rose up, and went to Ramah.

And we cannot talk about leadership impartation without mentioning the name of Moses. Moses' impartation was profound, dramatic, and intriguing. He visibly saw the Holy Ghost fire, and dramatically held the tail of a serpent:

> And Moses answered and said, But, behold, they will not believe me, nor hearken unto my voice: for they will say, the LORD hath not appeared unto thee. And the LORD said unto him, What is that in thine hand? And he said, A rod. And he said, Cast it on the ground. And he cast it on the ground, and it became a serpent; and Moses fled from before it. And the LORD said unto Moses, Put forth thine hand, and take it by the tail. And he put forth his hand, and caught it, and it became a rod in his hand.
> —Exodus 4:1–4

The Following Is a List of Five of the Major Leadership Styles in Practice

1. Laissez-faire Style (leader has no authority)
2. Democratic Style (group sets goals along with the leader)
3. Permissive Style (leader lets others worry about problems)
4. Autocratic Style (leader makes decisions and tells others)
5. Manipulative-Inspirational Style (leader sets goals and uses "hard sell" techniques with group)
6. Bureaucratic Style (group totally discouraged to participate in any way)

The Three Types of Leaders

There are generally three types of leaders: 1) The Self-made leader, 2) The Society-made leader, and 3) The God-made leader

The self-made leader

Self-made leadership is personal initiation into leadership. I need to clarify, however, that becoming a self-made leader is different from becoming a self-declared leader. To further clarify, assuming a title or credential does not make you a master or authority in that discipline. You can declare yourself a leader, but if you have not made yourself a leader, the self-declaration becomes a defeatist act.

The self-made leader is the leader who for the love, desire, aspiration and purpose of leadership symmetrically purposes, plans, programs, and pursues ideals that ultimately lead him into leadership status and office.

Thus the self-made leader was the one who went to work, trained, practiced, and was mentored, and eventually acquired what it took to become a leader.

This from secular management phraseology is innovation in pursuit of leadership skills for leadership. Pursuing academic excellence is a way of working yourself into a self-made leader, just as the pursuit of vocational training. It could be described then that all of life's aspirations have an accompanying element of self-made leadership.

Self-made leadership in general perspective appears to be the springboard for the other two leadership positions that have greater volumes of responsibilities.

For instance, society always looks forward to a person who already has acquired certain leadership values before they will fall on that person to assume leadership in its domain.

And even in the divine economy self-made leadership is one value God relishes in choosing the vessels for His work.

The society-made leader

Stephen was a perfect society-made leader. Being a society-made leader here means society chose you for some sort of leadership.

But as earlier indicated, society most often does not choose anybody for leadership within; society chooses somebody who has the qualities of a self-made leader when the need arises for societal responsibilities to be entrusted into the care of someone.

It was in this direction that Stephen and six other people were chosen by the multitude, based on certain leadership prescriptions by the apostles to serve in the business in ministry:

> Wherefore brethren, look ye out among you seven men of honest report, full of the Holy Ghost and wisdom, whom we may appoint over this business....And the saying pleased the whole multitude: and they chose Stephen, a man full of faith and of the Holy Ghost, and Philip, and Prochorus, and Nicanor, and Timon, and Parmenas, and Nicolas a proselyte of Antioch.
>
> —Acts 6:3,5

Stephen was one who climbed the ladder of progressive leadership. He was a self-made leader, then society picked him for responsibilities, and later he went on as a God-made leader, a Holy Spirit powerhouse as depicted in his famous sermon—the defense of Stephen captured in Acts 7. For brevity, we pick just one of his ministrations captured in Acts 6:8:

> And Stephen, full of faith and power, did great wonders and miracles among the people.

Leadership virtues are indispensable qualities that you need, society needs, and even God requires from us for the overall appreciation of humanity.

Before society would enthrone anyone a leader, the person will most likely be oozing with exquisite leadership qualities, for society will only enthrone someone who has already enthroned himself a leader, not by declaration but by acquisition.

Something merely declared goes into the air, evaporates, and is history; but something acquired stays with you; even when utilized there is always a reserve to call upon for future consumption.

The three-point requirements the apostles stipulated for Stephen and the other six men, and which is still an integral requirement in spiritual leadership and ministry, were: 1) Men of honest report, 2) Men full of the Holy Ghost, and 3) Men full of wisdom.

Laying out these leadership requirements for leaders which have a high dosage of "I am ready" virtues does not mean that people with dark blots on their records naturally become redundant in the leadership family. No, if ever a man had a background that would render him unusable to God, it was Paul.

Yet he became the greatest Christian worker to date, and his writings, the Pauline epistles have become the core of Christian beliefs and practices.

In reference to his dark blots, Paul writes in appreciation of the One who does the calling into spiritual leadership:

> And I thank Christ Jesus our Lord, who hath enabled me, for that he counted me faithful putting me into the ministry; Who was before a blasphemer, and a persecutor, and injurious: but I obtained mercy, because I did it ignorantly in unbelief.
>
> —1 Timothy 1:12–13

Leadership is best described by the following maxim: "God does not call the qualified to overqualify, He qualifies the unqualified."

Thus, the leader is always inadequate to fulfill the demands of leadership. Notwithstanding the saintly credentials with which we enter into ministry, we all need God's grace to be adequate in ministry.

The God-made leader

From the perspective that all humanity are the products of God, and society is a part of God's creation, it could be said that all leadership is God-made. But from the strictest sense, we shall categorize the God-made leader as the leader strictly chosen or made by God for a specific divine function.

The God-made leader is the servant of God, the leader called by God and anointed or empowered into ministry or a certain office for divine purpose. You might also not be far from correct to say that the God-made leader is the leader appointed by God into a certain office.

Most of the salutations of the Pauline epistles allude to a God-made leader, and we shall settle on 1 Corinthians 1:1:

> Paul called to be an apostle of Jesus Christ through the will of God, and Sosthenes our brother.

God-made leadership carries with it dualistic responsibilities—responsibilities from God, and reciprocal responsibilities from the called (you).

God's responsibilities in God-made leadership lie in His equipping and empowering the called leader so that in the course of his or her performances, God's name would not be blemished either by inaction or incompetence.

And the God-made leader's responsibility in the leadership bargain is to ensure that certain biblical virtues and ethics are inviolable in the course of their lives and in the discharge of their leadership functions.

Leadership responsibilities in this regard have some covenantal overtones. God has always been faithful in His covenantal relationships with humanity.

The problem has always been humanity breaking their part of this agreement, either overtly or covertly, and most often receiving punishment typical of the Samsonic experience in Judges 16:21:

> But the Philistines took him, and put out his eyes, and brought him down to Gaza, and bound him with fetters of brass; and he did grind in the prison house.

THE CALL OF MOSES

Any treatise on God-made leadership is incomplete without the name of Moses. Arguably the greatest leader that has ever walked on Earth (besides Jesus Christ, who was both divine and human), Moses' background was a blend of sublimation, splendor, and subjugation.

Moses' period of sublimation and splendor was the first forty years of his life, which were spent in the plush environment of the palace of Pharaoh.

And viewed from his strong contention for the throne, vis á vis his impeccable qualities that made him the cynosure of all eyes in the palace where he lived closer to Pharaoh in terms of facilities and reverence, the position of the next pharaoh was his for grabs.

But suddenly he found himself in the back side of the desert keeping the flock of Jethro, his father-in-law. And this highly educated man, who had been accustomed to the comforts and pleasures of the palace in subjugation, found himself occupying one of the lowest pursuits of his day—herding sheep. Indeed Moses saw his estate plummet so low to the point that he was working for his in-laws.

The Mosaic experience is one very central to leadership calling and training. Moses was not obsessed with bitterness in the desert; otherwise he would have missed the voice of God.

In leadership, especially in God-made leadership, our response to the clarion call must come only after we have heard the voice of God, or have the unquestionable conviction that we are headed towards God's calling for a certain function.

When someone asks you to serve in one way or another, make sure that God is in it. Do not jump into a ministry or leadership position on the whims of someone's prophecy when you are not in it.

In the Mosaic experience, God did not just speak to him, He revealed Himself as well to quash any uncertainty about Moses' calling:

> And the angel of the LORD appeared to him in a flame of fire out of the midst of a bush: and he looked, and, behold, the bush burned with fire, and the bush was not consumed.
>
> —Exodus 3:2

Leadership is about people, for people and not about money, which current ministry trends tend to portray. God has a burden for people and for the fulfillment of His purposes on Earth.

In calling people for leadership positions and functions, God looks for people already nursing similar burdens. God called Moses because Moses' burden for the Jews forced him into exile (earlier he had killed an Egyptian who was contending with a Hebrew, and out of fear for his life was forced to flee to the Midian desert).

And what about Paul? He was doing the right thing in a wrong way. He was defending the "truth," but was defending Judaism instead of the new movement, Christianity, which at the time had been newly founded by our Lord Jesus Christ.

God knew that both Moses and Paul were on the way, except that each needed an orientation or re-orientation to be able to do the right thing. Acts 9:15 gives a gist of Paul's orientation curriculum:

> But the Lord said unto him, Go thy way: for he is a chosen vessel unto me, to bear my name before the Gentiles, and kings, and the children of Israel.

It is worth reiterating that God, when calling people for leadership positions and functions, looks for people already nursing similar burdens. God called Moses because Moses' burden for the Jews forced him into exile. You must be in it before God will put you in it.

Leadership is about people, and about the burden for people. Without burden there will be no response from God, and without response from God there will be no leadership. God calls people into leadership out of His burden for situations and circumstances in people's lives.

All human leadership is from God, and all fruits and fulfillments of leadership's aspirations bring appreciation to humanity. This invariably gladdens God's heart, which primarily seeks to bring comfort and consolation to every heart, to every community, and to every nation.

And the satisfaction we experience when a job is well executed should goad all of us on into leadership responsibilities.

A Graph of Leadership with God-made Leadership as the Arrow Head

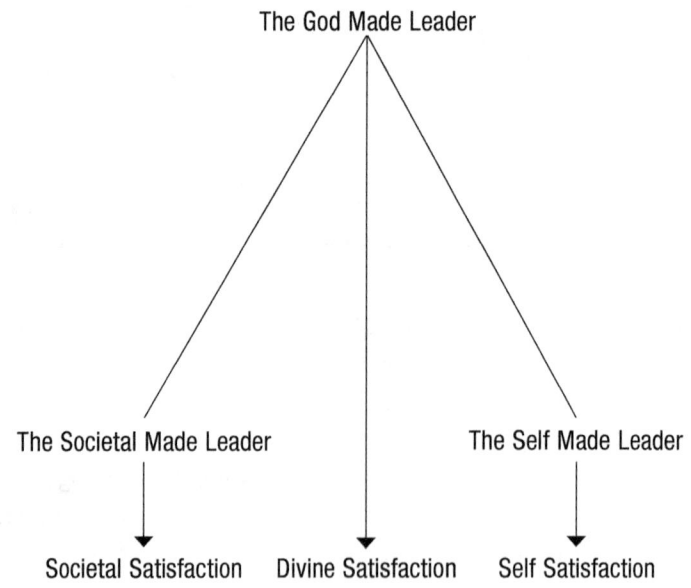

Chapter 17

THE STRATEGIC IMPACT OF STRUCTURAL AND INSTITUTIONAL FRAMEWORK WITHIN LEADERSHIP

LEADERSHIP IS A WORD with an overarching sphere of jurisdiction and influence.

Everything that has a vast sphere of influence certainly is, mildly put, divinely connected. Indeed, leadership's jurisdiction and influence goes further than being divinely connected. Leadership could be said to be one of the core attributes of God.

Creation bespeaks of God's ingenious leadership woven around structure and institution. This poignantly underscores the indispensability of structures and institutions within the framework of leadership, which, by conservative estimation, is as old as humanity within the perspective that humanity was attached to leadership right after its creation:

> And the LORD God took the man, and put him into the garden of Eden to dress it and to keep it.
>
> —GENESIS 2:15

Delving into the exegesis of the above scripture pointedly attaches leadership to humanity and underscores its indispensability both to humanity and to divinity.

Adam's first experience in the Garden of Eden was orientation in leadership *dress* and *keep*, which in today's leadership parlance is initiative and consolidation, or in a broader perspective leadership and management.

A treatise on leadership without its intractably woven mate, management, is a partial glimpse of the total picture. If the Father God did it pairing the two—dress (initiative/ leadership) and keep (consolidation/management)—then mortal and finite humanity cannot help but toe the line of the Being whose channel of connectivity (theology) is the father and mother of the arts and sciences, and the inspiration of all philosophies. And with the above hypothesis in place our inroad into leadership would unveil a holistic presentation.

Structural and Institutional Framework within the Church

The church is the cradle of leadership in human life and aspirations. Adam, the first human being, also was the first church, towing the memory lane of theology.

Adam's embodiment as the first church in human history had been given extensive coverage in the evolution of the church; the above is just a recap to emphasize the ageless nature of structural and institutional framework within the church.

Adam became the first leader in human leadership and management, two major machineries that work in tandem with structures and institutions towards delivery. Understanding the structures and institutions of management in general would lead to a better understanding of the structural and institutional framework within the church.

In plain language, structure and institution in management are the office and working machinery of a person in employment. Structures are crafted in or around the office or officeholders, and institutions serve as the working machinery through which the officeholder performs.

Structural Framework—The Fivefold Minister (Eph. 4:11)

- Question: What is structural framework within the church polity?
- Answer: A structural framework within the body polity of the church is a person or being who serves as a channel of order, and premise of jurisprudence in the administration of ministry duties in and for the church.

With the above definition as a guiding factor, the fivefold ministers become the prime structure in the church. Thus the structure becomes the body and status of leadership within the church as these offices were the first to be established by the Holy Spirit in the governance of the church:

> And he gave some, apostles; and some, prophets; and some, evangelists; and some, pastors and teachers.
>
> —Ephesians 4:11

The Fivefold Ministers as the Major Structures of the Church

Having cleared defined what serves as the constituents of the structures of the church—the fivefold ministers—we now zero in on a few aspects of what makes them the primordial and indispensable foundations of the structural component of the church:

- The church's hierarchical structure starts with the fivefold ministers (Eph. 4:11). The Holy Spirit appointed and empowered the fivefold ministers for the church with the maiden appointment on the day of Pentecost, and left the subsequent appointments and other related ministry appointments in their hands—from them to the next generation of leadership, and on and on.

- There is equipollence in the fivefold ministries. The apostle and the prophet however stand out as the prime movers of the structures in the polity of the church. And Ephesians 2:20–21 is a quintessential extract of this existential truth:

And are built upon the foundation of the apostles and prophets, Jesus Christ himself being the chief corner stone; In whom all the buildings fitly framed together groweth unto an holy temple in the Lord.

The importance of structures in the polity of the church structure unveils the depth of human resources in the church, and their placements and positions in its delivery process.

Structure in management helps to know the person or persons who are at the top, through to the middle-level personnel, to the person at the bottom of the process of delivery. The importance of structure in any enterprise is overarching:

1. Structures serve as the foundation for governance.
2. Structures make the entity discernible.
3. Structures aid in assessing and evaluating the human and material resources in an establishment.
4. Structures are facilitators for the accomplishment of goals of an establishment.
5. Structures lead to specialization, enhance performance, and ultimately increase growth in the sector.
6. Clearly defined structures and well-ordered institutions reduce to the barest minimum red tape-ism and bureaucracy, two key anti-growth and delivery mechanisms.

Structure—The Trinitarian Paradigm

In divine human relationship, God has revealed and/or manifested Himself to humanity, reflective of the theological concept that there are three Beings constituting the Trinity: the Father God, the Son God, and the Spirit God. Though it is said that there is equipollence in the Trinity, its composition is resplendent with structure. There sits atop the Father God, then comes the coronated Son God, and last but not least, the Holy Spirit, completing the order.

Order is relative to structure. Every ordered entity comes out of a well-defined structure; for there cannot be order without a structured entity behind it.

Humanity was created to perform, and creation was birthed for the same purpose. That is why there is so much order behind these two major works of the God of structure. This is a self-evident fact about the anatomy of humanity, and creation. Humanity has an embodiment of structure so as to be able to act in and around structure for its survival, underscoring the inevitable truth that one cannot live outside his source and the major factors that constitute him.

Establishing Structures in the Local Church—A Guide

Structures must be established in proportion to the size and vision of the church.

For instance, if you are constructing a single-story building you do not need a structural foundation meant for a skyscraper. That would amount to sheer waste of material and human resources. Similarly, a megachurch should have a megastructure tailored to meet its complex needs, whilst a small church must have a structure compatible to its administrative and institutional needs.

The following three major factors help determine the size of structures, and could add valuable weight to this treatise:-p The short-term, medium-term, and long-term goals should aid in the defining of the structures and establishment of the institutions respectively.

1. The available resources—human and material—should aid in determining the size and caliber of the extra human resources to employ, and the magnitude of the extra institutions to be established should reflect the present growth need of the entity.

Letting the Structures and Institutions Do the Work

Humanity is at the center of everything. Humans make and unmake; they build and destroy. In the "letting the structure do the work" milieu, the following benefits come in handy:

- Personalities do not count much here.
- Ego is a forgotten or barely recognized word.

The Strategic Impact of Structural and Institutional Framework Within Leadership

- Pursuit of individuals' agendas gives way to dogmatic adherence to the performance target set.
- Institutional culture becomes the prevalent culture within the entity.
- Discipline is always at the apex in well-structured entities, ultimately bringing about better performance.
- People work in compliance to structural order and in fulfillment of institutional targets. Accrual of optimum results is ensured under such a milieu.

STRUCTURES RELATIVE TO INSTITUTIONS IN THE FIVEFOLD MINISTRIES

STRUCTURES	INSTITUTIONS
The Apostle	The Apostolic Ministry
The Prophet	The Prophetic Ministry
The Evangelist	The Evangelistic Ministry
The Pastor	The Pastoral Ministry
The Teacher	The Teaching Ministry

INSTITUTIONAL FRAMEWORK—THE FIVEFOLD MINISTRIES (EPH. 4:12)

The relationship between the structural framework and the institutional framework within the polity of the church could be likened to the human anatomy. The human anatomy has the outer body (personage), and the inner body (the organs). The outer body projects the personage whilst the inner body does the real work, keeping the entire anatomy going.

By analogy the structural framework that projects the personage of the fivefold ministers is inhered by the institutional framework ministries that do the behind-the-scenes work.

Zeroing in on the institutional framework within the concept of the church, it is any body, organ, or machinery through which or by which the church is governed, or its functions carried out.

As the working channels of the top-echelon human resources of the church, the fivefold ministries become the major institutional frameworks in the church that produce a number of smaller institutions to supplement their managerial efforts.

The Purpose of Ministry

The purpose of ministry is threefold. Its primary purpose is to win souls into the church. Then the second purpose, an affiliate of the first, is to work on the growth, the maturity, and the responsibility capacities of the convert. And the third purpose, the ultimate of the work of the ministry—to provide corporate benefit to the entire body:

> For the perfecting of the saints, for the work of the ministry, for the edifying of the body of Christ.
> —Ephesians 4:12

The Fivefold Ministry as the Major Institution in the Church

As the major institutional machinery within the church, the tasks and responsibilities of the fivefold ministries are overarching and primordial. These come under four major summations.

1. It is the major policy-making house of the church

Policy formulation is the compass of any institution that leads it to its intended destination of fulfillment or accomplishment. Without policy any entity loses its sense of direction, focus of pursuit, agenda to fulfill, and the path to trail in life's aspiration.

With the above facts (or at least hypotheses) as a working tool relative to the importance of the institutional framework of ministry in the polity of the church, the importance of ministry in the overall functions of the church becomes even more profound.

The fivefold ministry's task as the major policy formulator of the church creates as well as crafts the long-term, medium-term, and short-term goals of the church. To this end, the fivefold ministries as the major policy house of the church ensures that this agelong policy acronym POLE becomes the working machinery of the church.

The word POLE in management principles is Plan, Organize, Lead, Evaluate. In proper policy there is planning. In proper policy organization, planning and organization are followed by processing and production. And in proper planning, evaluation subjects the production processes for redress and later strategizes for improved yield.

A Graph of Pole

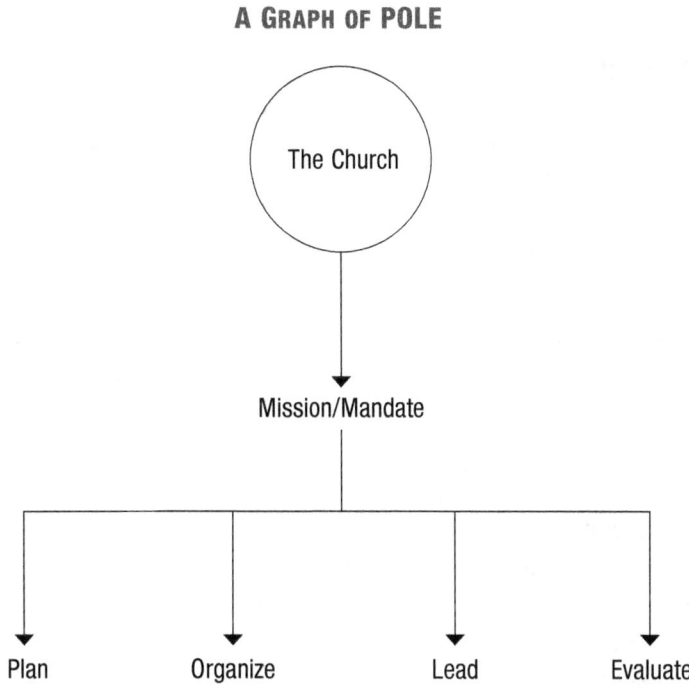

2. The functionality of the church revolves around them

The church has two identities—the spiritual identity and the physical identity. The spiritual identity of the church represents the organismic aspect of it, and the physical identity represents the organizational aspect. Both aspects must project great measure of functional qualities to reflect their billings as organismic and organization respectively.

It is for the functionality of the church that the presence and indispensability of the institutional framework of the church come in handy.

The church functions primarily on the liveliness of its institutional framework—the ministries of the fivefold. As the fivefold ministries function, the church functions; and as the church functions, ministry opportunities are created for all and sundry within the church, honing their individual organismic and organizational talents and giftings into a cohesive corporate force for the daunting work of ministry. Under such a milieu the synergistic power of ministry talent and gift is in full flight, as evidenced by the Pauline team that shook Ephesus during one of their countless evangelical adventures:

> And many that believed came, and confessed, and shewed their deeds.... So mightily grew the word of God and prevailed.
> —Acts 19:18,20

3. All the sub-ministries or departments in the church work around the visionary and policy direction of the fivefold ministries

Ministry itself operates from the top to the bottom, but the work of ministry starts at the bottom. This statement would appear paradoxical if the standard organizational chart of any corporate entity were to serve as a yardstick against the backdrop that it is leadership that decides what to do. But in real and practical operational issues, it is the implementation of the decisions made manifest through the fruits of the ordinary workers down the ladder who constitute the real work force, and whose output ultimately determines the economic gains of any entity, that counts. This does not seek to disdain the important role that leadership plays in any entity, but the above is vindicatory of the Pauline assertion made in Ephesians 4:12a:

> For the perfecting of the saints, for the work of the ministry.

4. It is the major organ in the church through which and by which other ministries are created

The church is the haven for divine human relationship, a home for brother/brother fellowship, and an edifice for ministry by those called into mainstream ministry, as well as those privileged to offer support services to the called.

This picture is better projected in the early part of the Old Testament priesthood, which had three compartments aside of the supplementary services provided by the tribal leaders and specially talented service providers. In the Old Testament priestly hierarchy, Moses was designated as God's spokesman to Aaron, and therefore to the entire Israelite people:

> And he shall be thy spokesman unto the people: and he shall be, even he shall be to thee instead of a mouth, and thou shalt be to him instead of God.
>
> —Exodus 4:16

Therefore, this scripture undoubtedly becomes the mirror that gives us a perfect image of the reason behind the Mosaic anointing in the annals of church history (our Lord and Savior Jesus Christ exempted, though, from the perspective that in the incarnate, God was walking and ministering among humanity).

Down the ladder of the priestly hierarchy, Aaron, the first high priest in human history, followed in that order, as is implied in this scripture:

> And he that is the high priest among his brethren, upon whose head the anointing oil was poured, and that is consecrated to put on the garments, shall not uncover his head, nor rend his clothes.
> —Leviticus 21:10

And God, respecting the principle of delegation in priestly management, appointed the sons of Aaron to serve in the office of the priest to be overseen by the father who was to serve as the high priest, as crisply presented in Leviticus 1:5:

> And he shall kill the bullock before the Lord: and the priests, Aaron's sons, shall bring the blood, and sprinkle the blood round about upon the altar that is by the door of the tabernacle of the congregation.

Further down the ladder, the tribe of Levi was separated from the twelve tribes of Israel exclusively for tabernacle duties to supplement the services of the priests, whose number was grossly insufficient for the extensive Old Testament tabernacle chores.

In the New Testament ministry and priestly setting, there appears to be a discernible connectivity to the structural framework of the Old Testament order that has been covered.

The five ministries serve as the high priestly office in the institutional framework of the church. These ministries, in our postmodern terminology, are the senior pastorate offices of the church.

Beyond the senior pastorate are the associate pastorate ministries, who offer invaluable supplementary and supporting services to the senior pastorate ministries. And further down the institutional ladder of New Testament church polity are the youth ministry, music ministry, and institutional ministries that oversee prison, hospital and other social ministries, depending on the size of the church.

In this elite era of the twenty-first century where specialization, excellence, and steep competition and dominance are the order of the day, any church that plays down the importance of institutional structure in the governance and administration of its vision and mission risks wallowing in mediocrity and obscurity. In climaxing the treatise, a modern-day linguistic presentation of structural and institutional framework as analogized below could be a pictorial and transparent projection.

The structural framework is the officeholder in the polity of the church, and the institutional framework is the office. The officeholder without an office to execute the tenants of his office renders that office existing on paper, whilst the existence of an office without an officeholder is tantamount to the graveside, where there are no living beings.

146 VARIEGATED TAPESTRY OF MINISTRY

The structural framework and the institutional framework, therefore, make the church.

A GRAPH OF THE STRUCTURAL FRAMEWORK OF THE OLD TESTAMENT PRIESTHOOD

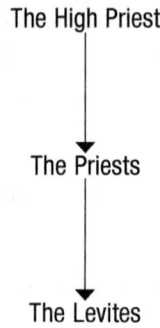

A TYPICAL STRUCTURAL FRAMEWORK OF A DENOMINATIONAL CHURCH

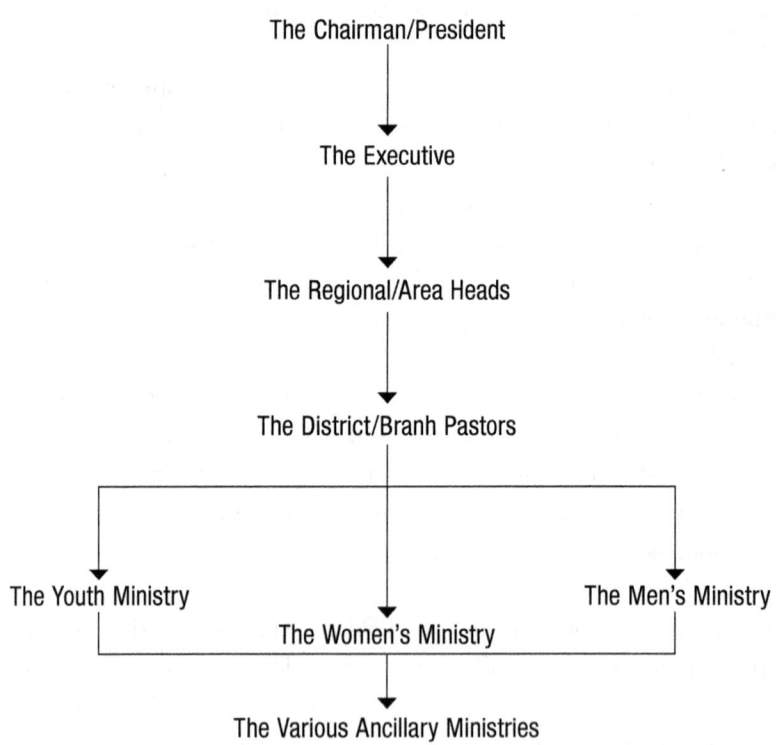

A TYPICAL STRUCTURE OF AN INDEPENDENT CHARISMATIC CHURCH

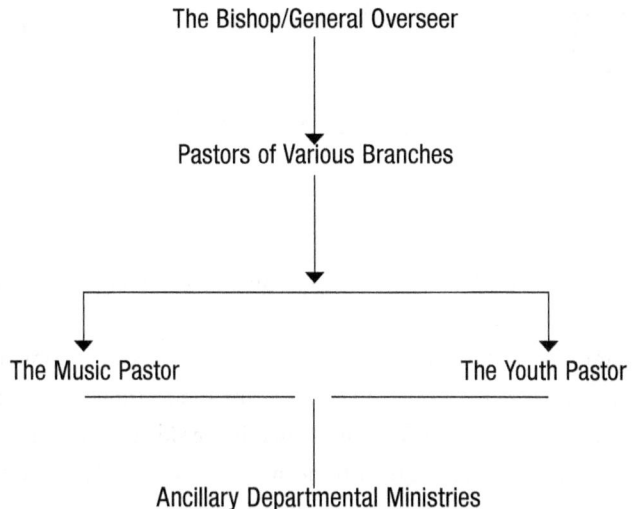

Chapter 18

VISION AND ITS PROCESSES OF ACTUALIZATION

VISIONS AND DREAMS ARE the two major vehicles that take great fulfillers and accomplishers to their destinations.

By their literary meanings, a dreamer is one who dreams, and a visionary is one who catches a vision. But there is another side of a dream and a vision within the context of expectancy, actualization, and fulfillment, which is the side under evaluation.

Though this treatise seeks to deal with the mental aspects and not the optical side of dream and vision, it shall nevertheless seek alliance with the optical aspect as recorded in Scripture, to strengthen and reinforce the relativity of the mental dimension to human accomplishment:

> And it shall come to pass afterward, that I will pour out my spirit upon all flesh; and your sons and your daughters shall prophecy, your old men shall dream dreams, your young men shall see visions.
> —JOEL 2:28

THE OLD DREAM

The exegesis of Joel 2:28 poignantly underscores the fact that dreams are for the old men and women in society.

Going by the above truth (or hypothesis), the present postmodern generation, which essentially is a generation of young men and young women, cannot toe the same line as previous generations, whose inspirational slogan was, "catch a dream."

Dreams belong to the old, thus the present young and enthusiastic generation cannot be the "I have a dream" generation; it must be the "I have caught a vision" generation.

VISION—MENTALLY

Having briefly unfolded the optical aspect of vision—catching a revelation, sometimes whilst semi-asleep—the focus now shifts to the mental aspect of vision. The Hebrew word *Khaw-zone* for vision, or sight (mentally) is very pertinent to the points of the treatise under address.

The mental aspect of vision is the compass that dogs the steps of great accomplishers in life. Similarly, the mental aspect of vision is the mental conception of the path of fulfillment one desires to pursue in life.

From another perspective, vision is the star that leads a person to his or her ultimate pursuit in life. A life therefore without vision, and to be accommodating without a dream (to relate to the generalized launching platform for life), is like content without form. That life can never meaningfully and profoundly touch society by its acts. For in life one needs to know what he opts before he can pursue meaningfully. You cannot go for anything tangibly ahead of you if there is nothing there. You must be pregnant with something before you can travail something; attempting to travail without pregnancy is an exercise in futility.

In life whatever a person produces is his or her "baby." And just as a baby cannot be produced or travailed without formation, a person who wants to accomplish must first be pregnant with that object of ultimacy in the "belly of the mind." Thus, the major accomplishment of a person's life is materialization of her vision.

Any living person without a vision to pursue or to guide his or her life is tantamount to a living dead. And to buttress this point, this extract from a Solomonic rendition via Proverbs 29:18a:

> Where there is no vision, the people perish.

RELATIVITY OF VISION TO THE PRESENT GENERATION

The impact of vision is overarching; it is relative to nations and their inhabitants, and to every stratum of society.

A nation without vision would shrink into oblivion among the comity of nations. An individual without vision would be left behind in today's "animal farm," survival-of-the-fittest-type environment. And any society without vision shall be the whipping boy of those whose visions are being realized through science, and are attempting a voyage to the moon to settle there once it is conquered.

Through vision, humanity's insatiable appetite for new products sees expansion day in and day out to their already expanded-to-near-explosion belly. But people keep on producing because vision seems to be in everybody's belly.

Joel 2:28 emphatically aligns vision with the person. And if today's population is predominantly a youthful one, then the fruits of vision would surely take the world to dizzy heights. With Joel 2:28 in retrospect, therefore, the world must be ready for an explosion in inventions, bringing home the point that vision is the bedmate of knowledge, which is increasingly abounding due to the closeness to the end of the lease period of the world:

> But thou, O Daniel, shut up the words, and seal the book, even to the time of the end: many shall run to and fro, and knowledge shall be increased.
>
> —Daniel 12:4

With the first commercial flight to the moon slated for next year, vision will have taken its astronomical feats to dizzying height once this becomes actualized. One may say that the present generation is the most privileged in terms of freedom from inhibition and anything that seeks to put brakes on one's desire of pursuit.

But it appears that unbridled freedom has its concomitant bedmate of moral decadence. Global morality is at an all-time low; consequently, society stinks. Ethical values have been thrown to the dogs, and humanity's behavior pattern today does not have any speck of dissemblance from jungle life. Shame is an unheard word in society, and the unbridled inalienable human rights philosophy permits anything, so long as self is ultimately satisfied.

The power of vision is so powerful that if allowed to operate without a curbstone, no one would be able to predict what man was capable of doing next.

"Catch a vision and pursue it to its logical end" surely must be the refrain of the day. However, the present unbridled generation must be curbed with reference to the Adamic checks and balance. Adam, not withstanding the vast power and authority given him by God, had a curbstone to guide him in his pursuit. Unfortunately, however, he sidestepped and fell into the bottomless pit of disobedience:

> And the Lord God commanded the man, saying, Of every tree of the garden thou mayest freely eat: But of the tree of the knowledge of good and evil, thou shalt not eat of it: for in the day that thou eatest thereof thou shalt surely die.
>
> —Genesis 2:16–17

The Source and Giver of Vision

Vision is a light in our mental faculty that crops up once in a person's life to give a sense of direction. That light is a fragment of the light of this world, which guides the whole world into the eternal presence of the Father God when it dawns. Jesus Christ is that Light of the world, and God is the Giver of vision, as well as its source:

> Then spake Jesus again unto them, saying, I am the light of the world: he that followeth me shall not walk in darkness, but shall have the light of life.
>
> —John 8:12

From the above apologetical stance, the sons and daughters of God must be the most visionary persons. The Christian, having been redeemed, recreated, and indwelt by God, becomes the latter's extension on Earth and also the prime receiver of the things of divinity.

This axiom is an integral part of the biblical truth that forms the foundational strata of our belief. This biblical truth is both experiential and revelatory, unlike Archimedean axioms, whose truth dwelt on empiricism.

Vision is good; Scripture emphasizes this in James 1:17, with regards to good things:

> Every good gift and every perfect gift is from above, and cometh down from the Father of lights, with whom is no variableness, neither shadow of turning.

If vision is good, and every good and perfect gift comes from God above, then vision is for constructive purpose, for everything born from heaven is preeminently for the good of humanity.

Vision, with its sublime productive ability, must not alienate us from God, as in the cases of highly gifted minds whose acts and deeds, the products of vision, have sought to be carried away by their intellectual and scientific accomplishments. These should have drawn them to God; for the things of God, in normal sequence, should draw us closer to their source, not alienate us from it.

Vision and Its Processes of Delivery

Vision is not a product, or the product. Vision is what takes a person to its product object in life if the various stages in the processes of vision were activated. The major stages in the travailing of vision are expatiated in their logical productive processes.

Vision Begets Goal

Goal is the ultimate desire, ambition, and intended destination of a person's life.

When God created humanity, He did so with a goal in mind: to have man preside over creation on His behalf. Therefore, humanity became the end of God's objective with regards to creation.

But a goal standing alone without certain additives to aid and propel it to fruition could be likened to wishful thinking, or an architectural design on the drawing board. Christianity's goal, for instance, is heaven. But when a person receives Christ, there are certain requirements to fulfill in order to actualize the goal of arrival in heaven during the Rapture.

This principle is equally applicable to our earthly life and aspirations. Our goal in life, birthed through the vision we catch, is only a means to an end, not an end in itself. And our goals, just like any means to an end, need collaboration and cooperative apparatus from compatible features to synergistically arrive at the end of the "goal."

A goal takes the fulfillment of the vision one catches a step closer to bringing that vision to fruition. It helps strengthen one's conviction base, which ultimately adds impetus to our confidence level. Confidence is an essential ingredient for success and accomplishment. Ask any person who made it in life when all odds were stacked against him of his hidden secrets, and he would tell you that confidence is one of them.

People who are confident are not afraid of failure, a monster that brings trepidation to first-timers and the faint-hearted. But to the confident, what seems like failure to others offers an opportunity for better output en route to conquering that which caused the setback.

Another essential feature that a goal brings to our natural development is that it adds Maccabean steel to our willpower. For the strength of our willpower is buoyed as the end result—the goal is glimpsed by our spirit.

And anybody aspiring to reach the goal of his or her life toes the line of discipline, an indispensable ingredient in the production process without which accomplishment remains a dream. The iconic Paul gives a gist of his secret—a high dosage of discipline:

> But I keep under my body, and bring it into subjection: lest that by any means, when I have preached to others, I myself should be a castaway.
> —1 Corinthians 9:27

Goal Begets Purpose

Purpose is variously defined in several dictionaries, but the terms I picked to aid us are *design* and *aim*. To design is to create something for further development towards an intended objective. Snappily put, we design for a purpose. And we design towards a perceived objective. In this wise, goal begets purpose for design, to help it (goal) to get where it (goal) is intending to go.

The next rung of the definition of purpose is *aim*. Having an aim is being specific about the exact target one attempts to hit. Without specificity, one's aiming at an object would amount to an effort in futility.

Great archers are those who are dogmatic in specificity; a mentality of laser-guided specificity makes a great archer. People of purpose moving towards their avowed goal in life therefore must have this archery principle to help them see the end of the tunnel of their life's goal. And again Paul, a man you cannot ignore in terms of reference for pursuit of life's aspiration, offers valuable tuition and counseling:

> I therefore so run, not as uncertainly; so fight I, not as one that beateth the air.
>
> —1 CORINTHIANS 9:26

Paul's tutorial here, both in precision and in perspicuity, has an element of denotative and connotative attachment. "So fight I" denotes an object in mind, and "not as one beateth the air" connotes perspicuity. So then, our purpose towards our goal in life must be pursued with a marriage of precision and perspicuity.

PURPOSE BEGETS DIRECTION

Precision in perspicuity is always towards a direction. Life is full of options, and there are several beckoning directions to choose from. The direction a person takes in life in pursuit of purpose towards an intended goal determines the *when* and the *how* of life's success or failure stories.

When the *Habiru* people left Goshen, the purpose was loud and manifest (to come out of slavery) and the goal crystal clear (to go to a land overflowing with milk and honey).

They had two options—avert the Red Sea and go by a shorter route, or go by the Red Sea to elongate the journey—though God did the choosing. But when it came to what direction to pursue to the Promised Land, the Red Sea was their prerogative. They had to choose between the directions of faith and trust in the Lord before them and that of fear and rebellion, respectively of the inhabitants on the land and against God. They took the latter option and the result is history: none of the first generation Exodus team, save Joshua and Caleb, possessed the Promised Land. Their rebellion against God was so pervasive that Moses, of all people, was caught in the spillover of their acts, necessitating his inability to step on the Promised Land:

> And the LORD spake unto Moses that self same day, saying, Get thee up into this mountain Abarim, unto mount Nebo, which is in the land of Moab, that is over against Jericho; and behold the land of Canaan, which I give unto the children of Israel for a possession: And die in the mount whither thou goest up, and be gathered unto thy people.
>
> —DEUTERONOMY 32:48–50

The bane of Moses was the direction the Jews took towards their intended destination in life, a land overflowing with milk and honey. Their choosing the direction of fear and rebellion, which was not endorsed by God, was the undoing of Moses. The greatest leader of all time (besides our Lord Jesus Christ, because essentially He is God) was derailed by a single decision; out of frustration, anger, and despair, he struck the rock twice contrary to the divine fiat of a solitary strike.

Leadership is great and glorious, but has its other gloomy side if the game is not played to the prescription of the overlord of divine leadership—God. The leader must learn to listen to God, especially when it matters most.

Direction Begets Focus

Focus is the anchorman in the delivery process of vision. And as every anchorman appears to be the strongest and/or the best among the starters, at least hypothetically, so is focus among the vision-fulfilling crew. And the spiritually effervescent Paul could not do it without "him" focus, as this glimpse of the secret behind his success, extracted from the intellectually laden Scriptures below unveil:

> Wherefore seeing we also are compassed about with so great a cloud of witnesses, let us lay aside every weight, and the sin which doth so easily beset us, and let us run with patience the race that is set before us, Looking unto Jesus the author and finisher of our faith; who for the joy that was set before him endured the cross, despising the shame, and is set down at the right hand of the throne of God.
>
> —Hebrews 12:1–2

In a world dominated by overly intrusive commercial apparatuses that sometimes cause one to commit to a product he had not previously budgeted for, one would have to firmly stick to his agendas for life or be veered off by equally diverting tendencies controlling the five senses of humanity.

Focus, the last leg in the visionary processes, is a reassuring environment. It is at the end of what had been labored for years.

Being within the reach of accomplishment is different from having accomplished. Many have seen their labors and efforts evaporate before the moment of possession when the powers against fulfillment struck.

Our Lord and Savior Jesus Christ is a perfect case study. For nearly thirty-three years, He knew about and ministered towards His ultimate death on the cross. But just at the dying embers of fulfillment, He made a final appeal to His Father:

> And he was withdrawn from them about a stone's cast, and kneeled down, and prayed, Saying, Father if thou be willing, remove this cup from me: nevertheless not my will, but thine, be done.
>
> —Luke 22:41–42

That Jesus Christ our Savior of all had to refocus through divine Fatherly intervention shows the intensity of warfare around the "medal zone" of fulfillment. We all fall prey to the "monster" of focus diversion, but the unalloyed assurance from the Trinity to see us through is always fulfilled when it matters most, as was the case when Jesus received strength through angelic reinforcement:

> And there appeared an angel unto him from heaven, strengthening him.
> —LUKE 22:43

The time is short, the prize is within reach, and the whole of heaven is on its feet to applaud as you are within reach of touching the reality of your vision; stretch out and possess it, for the glittering crown of accomplishment awaits you in heaven.

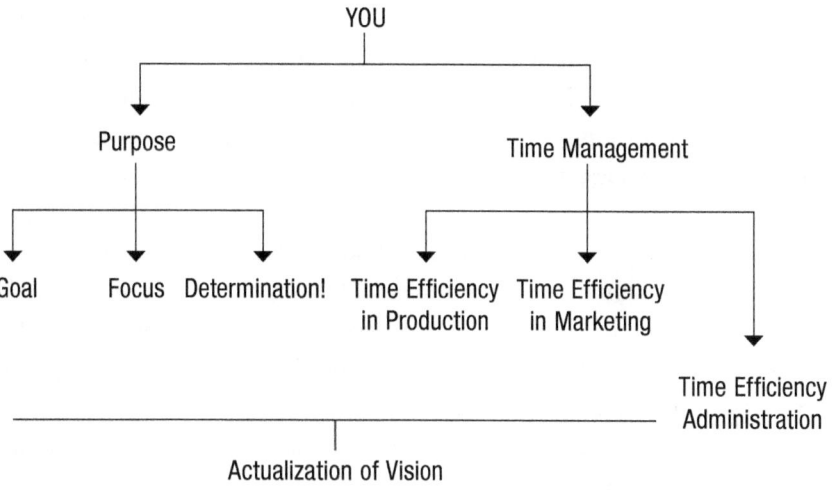

Chapter 19

THE JOSHUAIC LEADERSHIP PARADIGM

JOSHUA WAS AN EPOCH-MAKING leader who burst onto the scene after the sudden departure of his mentor, Moses, arguably the greatest leader of all time and whose shoes Providence beckoned him to step into.

Stepping into the shoes of a great leader is a tall order, but stepping into the shoes of one whom Divinity elevated above the human pedestal becomes an almost impossible task, from human perspective. Therefore, if Joshua succeeded in stepping into the shoes of Moses (which he did, and in admiration too), then there were certain undercurrents behind his success story as a leader of immense proportions. His story is a dominant feature in any documentary of the greatest leaders that ever walked on this earth, biblically and secularly.

No theology, they say, is without a context. And it is also generally believed that there is an unseen power behind every great leader within a generation. If these hypotheses are anything to go by, then it must added that every great leader leaves behind a legacy to become paradigmatic of leadership. In this light, the Joshuaic leadership paradigm becomes a benchmark for aspiring leaders via theology and the Bible.

Thus several paradigmatic leadership principles evolve from the Joshuaic studies to inspire and guide present and future leaders, at least from the biblical stock. Joshua 1:1–11 therefore comes under microscope exegesis:

1. "MOSES MY SERVANT IS DEAD," V. 2
(LEADERSHIP IS PROGRESSIVE)

"Moses my servant is dead" carries both connotative and denotative implications.

Messages to us in the connotative sense bring home the reality of the information in the literary sense. And relative therefore to the text under evaluation, God told Joshua that Moses, his mentor, was dead; Moses was not going to come back to life to lead the Jews again. From the hermeneutical perspective, it was a connotative message in a parabolic presentation.

Leadership is about wisdom. Anybody who opts for leadership or steps into leadership must have it before any other thing. In leadership parlance, it is the indispensable antecedent:

> Wisdom is the principal thing: therefore get wisdom: and with all thy getting get understanding.
> —Proverbs 4:7

There is an element of commonality among great leaders that have caressed the planet, leaving indelible imprints for future generations. The common element is wisdom. Thus, behind the denotative meaning of the theme under addressal, God was teaching Joshua some principles of wisdom via parabolic presentation, to enjoin the centrality of wisdom with His message.

Then the primary denotative emblem in the divine release, "Moses my servant is dead," was to let Joshua forget about the past, when he walked in the shadow of Moses. And the second deduction from the message was for Joshua to recognize that the mantle of leadership to take over from Moses had fallen on him.

In life's journey there is always a time for mentoring, and a time to graduate from mentorship. Life is about graduation; you live at one level for some time, and then another level at another time, and so on and so forth. Whosoever lived at one level indefinitely in a lifetime, spiritually, mentally or physically, never deployed fully the potential that was in him or her. And this situation is tantamount to subjecting one's productive organs to one-dimensional circled menu.

Humanity is an entity prone to change; we are clustered by ecological and elemental patterns of frequent change. We therefore have to live in consonance with the powers at work in our environment.

Leadership is dynamic, and everything infused with dynamism is a changing tool. Great leaders were advocates of change who called for and saw massive changes in the structures they came to meet; they threaded areas others could not dare, unveiled the unknown and conquered it, to give us cause to go through the memory lane of leadership.

2. "Now," v. 1a
(The Potential Leader Must Know the Moment of Reckoning to Step into Leadership When It Comes)

Knowing is one thing; knowing and reacting is another thing. When you know and do not change, you add nothing to your stature or your estate.

It is said that Napoleon Bonaparte once pointed to a map of China and said, "There lies a sleeping giant. If it ever wakes up, it will be unstoppable." Today China is unstoppable; it is unstoppable because it is awake. But China as a giant country did not just get up one day and say, "I am dead so I need to wake up." It took a leader to propel China toward becoming the economic powerhouse it is today and bringing a paradigm shift into the global economic dynamics.

Who therefore could begrudge the idolized Chairman Mao Tse Tung, whose name could almost be considered as a religion in China, the leader who masterminded the wake-up "revelation" of this vast country whose potential, I believe, is yet to be fully tapped.

In the "Now," the intimation was for Joshua to know that his moment of reckoning had come; he needed to react appropriately and step into the shoes of Moses, his idolized mentor.

Every society is the cause of an effect; and as such, society does not make itself, somebody makes it. Then someone has to be the anchor head, which inferentially is the leadership. The leader's position in society and in the divine economy comes into prominence, both on behalf of God and the overall good of that society, which becomes their first point of communal contact.

3. "Therefore Arise," v. 2b (Admonishes the Release of all Your Leadership Potential, Skill and all the Inherent Qualities Imbedded in You)

The potential in humanity, from the days of Adam till date, has barely been utilized. Mildly put, there is desuetude in the human potential.

Humanity has been the worry of divinity from the time of creation to date. Adam could not help us with a smooth takeoff to kingdom lifestyle. When he was expected to rule, he allowed himself to be ruled by Satan, transferring the ownership of the world to him. And Satan's statement in Luke 4:5–6 is an implicit expression of this fact:

> And the devil, taking him up into a high mountain, shewed unto him all the kingdoms of the world in a moment of time. And the devil said unto him, All this power will I give thee, and the glory of them: for that is delivered unto me; and to whomsoever I will give it.

Psychologists say that on the average we use just two percent of the potential of the human brain, to the chagrin of the Creator God. If God had wanted us to use just two percent of the capacity of our brain, He would have given us a brain with that two-percent capacity.

Thus when the opportunity arose for God to choose a replacement for Moses, He had to charge the then reclusive and intrepidly wanting Joshua to arise and take charge, for he was the only person to do so.

In life, many were those who caught the vision, and many were those who were presented with fabulous opportunities yet never saw the end of the tunnel of accomplishment. Their bane? They did not see or realize the "therefore arise" moment in their lives.

In life, there is always a "therefore arise" moment. When that moment passes by without notice, forget about achieving celebrity status. You will end up as an also-ran.

4. "Over This Jordan," v. 2c (Anything that Tries to Tower over You and to Intimidate You, Especially Before Your Maiden Undertaking in Life/Ministry)

When God told Joshua to "go over this Jordan," He was trying to pump out the adrenaline in him. This action was successful; Joshua did not waste time in instructing the leaders and captains to get the people prepared for the takeoff to conquer Jordan.

In leadership, a crisis period demands quick response cloaked in razor-sharp zeal; Joshua lived up to this billing.

When Obama took office in the White House, the U.S. economy was in tatters, and almost on the brink of collapse. Obama's emergence on the scene could be likened to Joshua's—both assumed leadership roles at a young age.

And just as Joshua commanded in haste to ready the people for the conquest of the Jordan, upon his assumption of office Obama didn't blink an eye before unleashing the economic stimulus package plan which today largely accounts for the gradual recovery of the United States economy, and whose spill over was felt along every nook and cranny of the globe, though current events seem to be eroding that.

Leadership is about taking action and rising to your billing, vis á vis challenges of leadership. Any leader whose stock of trade was passing the buck was not fit to assume the tag of leadership in the first place. Leadership is not about raking the "Goliaths" of the past. Leadership is not about shying away from realities. Leadership is not about chickening out when faced with challenges; instead, leadership is about releasing the "super eagle" in you when confronted with challenges.

Leadership is not about shying away from realities when they come your way. Remember, shying away from reality does not cause reality to shy away from you; it will meet you head-on in the direction you choose to escape from it.

And in His divine fiat to Joshua, God in His own Word said "Over this Jordan," denoting unrecognition of the Jordan River, the challenge facing Joshua.

Every leader must first acquire what it takes to lead. And having acquired what it takes to lead, you must be in a position of confidence to tell any challenge that comes your way that *greater is He that is in me than this challenge that confronts me*. And to the Christian leader, the maiden Johannine epistle provides an extra fillip:

> Ye are of God, little children, and have overcome them: because greater is he that is in you, than he that is in the world.
>
> —1 John 4:4

5. "Every Place that the Sole of Your Foot," v. 3a (Leadership Is About Making Inroads and Adding New Leadership Principles to What One Came to Meet)

God was the first leader, and the one who taught Moses. His first leadership alphabet exudes leadership principles far above human comprehension. The above statement of Joshua on the peripheral appears to be a statement of promise, but behind are profound and legend-making principles to be discovered if the spirit of revelation graciously unveils them to you.

In "every place the sole of your foot shall tread upon" emerges the first principle enclosed above, which I will term "the blank check" in the dynamics of leadership. The inference is that every leadership position with which one is graciously entrusted has a one-digit number; the recipient is given the option to fill in any desirable number. In this wise, whatever figure you put behind the one-digit figure on the check becomes your area of conquest and your contribution to leadership enhancement.

The above assertion is very relevant to the commandment or promise under addressal, for "everywhere the sole of your foot shall tread" refers to uncharted territory awaiting demarcation by the stroke of one's pen, or acts of leadership heroism.

Second, humans, by nature of their complex makeup, are very enigmatic. And as dynamism is ingrained in complexities, so is humanity. The complex nature of humanity brings out the dynamic traits in them, and this creates the spillover effect of insatiability, with their demanding tastes always craving new things. This inherent trait, very reflective in every sphere of human endeavor, encapsulates leadership principles too.

Thus by the principle under addressal, the leader should have the penchant to unravel new leadership principles, both in ministry and in secular leadership practices.

The adventurous leader must not harbor fear or hesitate to be adventurous in pursuit. Remember that the known was unknown until somebody decided to be adventurous and conquered it.

The good leader is not the leader who toes the tradition of the status quo for results.

The good leader is the person who, when confronted with emerging and sophisticated challenges akin to the new postmodern world of sophistry, emerges contemporaneously with his or her own leadership crafting and ingenuity to put to sleep the problem.

Two leadership personalities emerge within the leadership theme under address: 1) The leader who is a troubleshooter, and 2) The leader who is able to develop the vaccine to treat the "encroached virus."

- The leader who is a troubleshooter has the hawk's eye in leadership. This leader is able to spot a leadership challenge or obstacle afar, devise the right weapon, and club it down before it enters his territory. From another perspective, they are the leaders with the "patriot missiles" on their leadership borders.
- The leader who is able to develop the vaccine to treat an "encroached virus" is the leader who, when overtaken by a challenge in leadership, is able to counter it with well-strategized leadership methodology and eliminate the virus.

The first class of leaders includes great and admirable leaders of foresight, and the secondary category of leaders are those with a bottomless depth of leadership skills.

6. "Shall Tread Upon," v. 3b
(Leadership Principles Are Dynamic Thus the Leader Should have the Penchant to Unravel New Leadership Principles in Ministry)

Assertiveness

Every leader must know when to assert himself and when to play diplomacy.

Stepping on toes is a necessary evil in leadership. No good leader consciously decides to step on toes, but in the enforcement of leadership values the leader cannot help but step on some toes due to the psychological, emotional and other inherent differences in humanity. However, the good leader is the one who, after stepping on some toes, is able to woo the stepped-on toes to his or her side for a united pursuit of the objective at hand.

There are two types of assertiveness relative to this theory: result-oriented assertiveness and personality-orientated assertiveness.

The result-oriented assertiveness

In good leadership practices, the principles overshadow any other factor. This dovetails into the result-oriented assertiveness, in which principles become the central objects of pursuit and enforcement. The objective value and fulfillment of the principle becloud the "ballplayers" on the team.

This practice does not in any way reduce the placement and influence of the structural framework in place. The principles in any establishment work in tandem towards the fulfillment of the corporate goals, and structure is enhanced and strengthened.

The personality-oriented assertiveness

In leadership, principles work only when there are personalities behind them. Principles are made for humanity, but humanity is not made for principles. This unequivocally underscores the preeminence of humanity in any governing structure. Consequently, the assertiveness of personalities within the strata of production becomes a matter of course.

The effective leader must be able to assert the principles within the establishment or entity, and top up with a reasonable measure of personality assertiveness. The leader must have a posture of reasonable influence to be able to lead as well as draw people to their side. The leader who is reasonably assertive does not operate under much anxiety. The assertive leader is not timid. Exaggeration and bragging is not the stock of trade of an assertive leader. Over-sensitivity, self-criticism, depression, and difficulty in making decision, the fruits of low self-esteem, are not traits of the assertive leader, for whom high self-esteem is an integral quality.

Therefore, in leadership there must be a marriage of assertiveness of principles and assertiveness of personality for optimum results.

7. "FROM THE WILDERNESS AND THIS LEBANON," V. 4A THE STARTING)...UNTO THE GREAT SEA (POINT OF FULFILLMENT)

Leadership is about fulfillment, and in fulfillment there is always a starting point. Thus fulfillment is analogous to a journey. And as every journey has a starting point and an end, so has fulfillment a starting point and an ending point.

When God gives you a commission, He shows you the boundaries thereof. He does not commission and leave you to wallow in the boundaries of uncertainty.

Joshua's starting point of conquest and possession was "the wilderness and this Lebanon." Within this direction lies a pervasive leadership principle: anyone in pursuit of vision and fulfillment must have a starting point.

When a person starts the journey of life or fulfillment, they know exactly where they are going, what they need to get there, how long it is going to take to get them there, and what is at the end of the journey.

8. "Toward the Going Down of the Sun," v. 4c (Expansion of Vision)

Fulfillment is about actualizing a vision. A vision, as discussed earlier, is the primary objective of life. Vision is elastic and expansible. "Toward the coming down of the sun," implies a boundary or an end without demarcation. This was the description God gave Joshua to determine the end of the vast land he was to conquer and share among the Israelites.

Humanity is an unstoppable being; unstoppable within the purview of the unlimited power and authority vested in it during creation, and unstoppable from the perspective of the vast and unending potential and of the power of the brain. Genesis 1:28 will suffice:

> And God blessed them, and God said unto them, Be fruitful, and multiply, and replenish the earth, and subdue it: and have dominion over the fish of the sea, and over the fowl of the air, and over every living thing that moveth upon the earth.

An American president is sworn into office as the president and leader of the United States. His boundary of jurisdiction is the four corners of the United States. But any American president who desired to rule the world could do so through diplomatic, political and military ingenuity, without necessarily seeking the endorsement of every American. This is leadership power for you, via the principle of the fullest deployment of potential.

When you are in leadership, there is a designated area of operation for you. But if your leadership is good, you can extend its influence beyond what was originally earmarked for you, depending upon the magnitude by which you deploy the leadership potential in you.

Adolf Hitler came to power in Germany, added much of Europe to it, and decided to go for the whole world until he was stopped in his tracks by a global coalition force. The Germans did not vote for him to conquer Europe and the world; he decided to do it because he felt he had enough military clout to do so. That's an example of leadership by taking territories without your jurisdiction for you.

Kwame Nkrumah became the first president of Ghana, having conquered the British and broken their colonial hegemony over Ghana. Nkrumah was not content, and decided to go for the whole of Africa with that intention clothed in his declarative statement during Ghana's Independence proclamation, taken from the Ghana National archives:

> The Independence of Ghana is meaningless until it is linked up with the total liberation of the African continent.

And who says Kwame Nkrumah was not successful in his pursuit? At the time he was overthrown through a coup d'etat, which Africans believe was masterminded by the imperialist powers, almost the entire continent was breathing political freedom. And this man ended up becoming Africa's man of the last century.

Great leaders in history were those who extended their domain of influence beyond their frontiers. And leadership beckons you to step into their shoes.

9. "There Shall Not Any Man Be Able to Stand Before Thee," v. 5 (Divine Attachment to His Mission)

The calling of God is not an estate of isolation. There are additives to divine calling. And God's additives to His calling at least ensure that there is a factor of the theophanic manifestation amidst humanity, debunking the misconception that God does not "monkey" the world. The world belongs to God, and thus He does not indefinitely leave it ajar for the powers of evil to have a field day.

Any leader put there by God has His empowerment as back-up support. God empowers any person He calls even before commissioning, and Acts 2:2–4 is a quintessence:

> And suddenly there came a sound from heaven as of a rushing mighty wind, and it filled all the house where they were sitting. And there appeared unto them cloven tongues like as of fire, and it sat upon each of them. And they were all filled with the Holy Ghost, and began to speak with other tongues, as the Spirit gave them utterance.

The church as the embassy of God, and its congregants as the ambassadors of God with the fivefold ministers as the prime ambassadors, was adequately resourced on its inauguration on the Day of Pentecost. The Trinity did not leave anything to chance in this respect (see Acts 2:1–4; Ephesians 4:8–12).

But aside of the corporate anointing on the church and on the fivefold ministers, God empowers any person given a special assignment with the commensurate anointing and wisdom needed for the accomplishment of the given task.

Again, in ministry and in special leadership, God accompanies His mission with assurances to the person; He commits that special task through revelation, the *rhema* word, verbal communication, or any other means He chooses.

The backup anointing and ability God gives to people He calls into leadership is one of the assured biblical truths.

10. "I Will Be With Thee: I Will Not Fail Thee, nor Forsake Thee," v. 5b (God's Weight Behind Us)

Christian leadership is not for those who want to stay in the comfort zone of Christianity. Neither has Christian leadership a room for those who don't like challenges, trials, temptations and tribulations. But notwithstanding all the associated tribulations of Christian leadership, the "Bema" of Christ offers us great aspiration, hope, courage, and assurance to plod on. There can be no crown without the precedence of a "cross," therefore the associated problems of Christian leadership represents our cross to the crowns.

When challenges confront us in Christian leadership to a breaking point, we must be encouraged by Yahweh's assurances to Joshua. Just as He stood by Joshua, so shall He stand behind us. Remember that the calling, gifting, and commissioning of God are without variations, at least by the primary principles of divine calling and sustenance.

11. "Be Strong," v. 6 (Mobilizing Your Inner Strength)

The real strength of humanity is hidden within the various organs that inhere them. Therefore whatever strength any person exudes from the outer is just a fraction of the vast strength hidden in their arsenals within.

Naturally every person is imbued with strength—inner, i.e., mental, willpower, and outer, which manifests through our outer embodiments. Then when we are born again by the divine power injected into the recreated human spirit, we become people beyond the ordinary.

Further, any person commissioned into spiritual leadership goes through ceremonial anointing, which invariably turns him into a different person, with the supernatural in vogue whenever duty beckons him into action:

> Then Samuel took the horn of oil, and anointed him in the midst of his brethren: and the Spirit of the Lord came upon David from that day forward. So Samuel rose up, and went to Ramah.
> —1 Samuel 16:13

But having the strength is one thing, and releasing or deploying that inner strength when the need demands—that is another thing.

The magnitude of one's strength is only seen when deployed. Therefore, God, in enjoining Joshua to be strong, was reiterating the fact that he should release his inner strength for the task at hand.

A true leader is the one who is strong in the spirit and in the mind, and has also fine-tuned his body to reflect the strength within.

Leadership accomplishment is collaborative. God's responsibility is to strengthen or empower you from the outside to supplement your naturally imbedded human strength. Your responsibility in leadership is to call on the inner and the outer strength, by way of the divine impartation to confront whatever challenges that come your way.

12. "Be of a Good Courage," v. 6b
(Courage Comes Within You, Know What Is Within)

In a world dominated by what influences the five senses, courage is a scarce commodity. Strength and courage are bedmates, as well as partners in performance; one does not go without the other in accomplishment. Courage is like a vertical object that stretches itself taller than a confronting situation, and beckons strength to coil around for release to quash whatever challenge stands before them.

Saul and David make perfect case studies here. When Goliath stood before the Israelites, Saul as the king could have put Goliath to sleep by virtue of the anointing that was on him. Remember, both Saul and David were anointed by the prodigiously gifted Samuel. The difference between them was that while Saul chickened out, David chuckled at the "prey" that was before him and went for it. That marked the methodical rise of the legendary king David, arguably Israel's most successful king.

13. "Shalt Thou Divide For An Inheritance," v. 6c
(Leadership Is Being a Blessing to Others)

Leadership is about fulfilling a purpose, and sharing your success with others. Every good leader's obsession therefore is the people he serves or leads, and not what he could realize for himself out of his position. This is the hallmark of great achievers.

The man who produced the first airplane, and whose product facilitated aeronautical excellence is dead and gone. Today, we are the beneficiaries of the stress and strain of somebody. This is leadership. Leadership is about production, not for oneself but for the society at large.

When Joshua conquered the nations entrusted to his conquest and divided the booty, he did not take a chunk of the territories for himself. That was true leadership at its finest.

When a leader's attention is on self, his or her products don't outlive the person's life span. When such leaders produce, they produce for self, and when they die their products die with them.

Great leaders are leaders of foresight. When a leader is for self he does not see far. But when a leader is for others, he sees the last person in his perspective afar, with another person emerging, and on and on. Under such a milieu, fresh challenges emerge to reflect the dynamic and unique nature of human values and aspirations.

And in true Christian leadership, the acronym *JOY* is always in resplendent view: Jesus first, Others second, and You last.

Chapter 20

THE DANIELIC HIGH-PROFILE LEADERSHIP PREREQUISITES (DAN. 1:4–8)

DANIEL WAS AN EXTRAORDINARY character—you could come up with several adjectives to befit him. A person of Daniel's caliber appears once in perhaps five hundred years. In brief, Daniel was a puritan, a Nazarene, a perfectionist, a vegetarian, a "prayeraholic," and an apologist.

The Book of Daniel has its fair share of theological divide when it comes to canonization against the backdrop of views held by certain liberal scholars and modern philosophical assumption that long-range predictive prophecy is impossible. This is reflective of the enigmatic figure of Daniel.

Daniel was a leader of unassailable qualities. The secret behind his leadership success is divided into its component parts and analyzed below to give us a clear idea of who he was. Daniel 1:4–8 is the text from which we will extract these Danielic leadership principles:

1. PURITY AND HOLINESS ("CHILDREN IN WHOM WAS NO BLEMISH," V. 4A)

In ministry, the character formation of the minister must precede his charismatic empowerment. Character formation is of far more importance than charismatic empowerment. Today, however, the craving for charismatic empowerment and knowledge is preeminent; character has been dumped into the dustbin. Today all types of characters mount the podium and dish out homilies to the unsuspecting parishioners, who accept what they hear as long as the homilies are delivered with intellectual and technical finesse (and sometimes sophistry).

In ministry, the minister's greatest weapons are holiness and purity. The ministry is God's ministry, and therefore everything done for God must be reflective of His attributes, of which holiness and purity are an integral part. You cannot be ungodly and do the work of God; evil and sin don't collaborate. God loves the sinner but hates sin. God redeems the sinner and helps him to overcome sin.

Ministry is about power and empowerment. But these can only fall into place if the minister first draws close to God and maintains a relationship with Him, as Hebrews 12:14 quintessentially records:

> Follow peace with all men [and women], and holiness, without which no man shall see the Lord.

A background check of all the great men and women in Scripture who were mightily used by God would reveal two common elements in their lives: holiness and purity. The ministries of those who did not toe this line ended catastrophically. Samson readily comes to mind in this respect, as he disdained his Nazarene vows, visited prostitutes, and was blinded prior to his death (see Judges 16:21).

2. GLORIOUS PERSONAGE ("WELL FAVORED," V. 4B)

The glory of God is one of the pervasive theophanic manifestations of Yahweh. God's *kabod*, His glory or majesty, induces an element of appearance which catches the eye. This glory covered Mount Sinai, and Moses, when he reached the summit to interact with God and to receive the Ten Commandments:

> And Moses went up into the mount, and a cloud covered the mount.
> —EXODUS 24:15

Anybody genuinely called by God into ministry is an associate of God. And every associate of God is a carrier of a theophanic manifestation. Therefore, the glory of God is upon the called both generally and ministerially. In this light, the seal of God as mentioned in 2 Corinthians 1:22 is a glimpse of the theophanic manifestation:

> Who hath also sealed us, and given the earnest of the Spirit in our hearts.

3. PRUDENCE AND VERSATILITY ("SKILLFUL IN ALL WISDOM, AND CUNNING IN KNOWLEDGE," V. 4C)

A gift is imparted, but skill is acquired. In leadership, no matter how gifted one might be, skill is always needed to blend what is celestially received with what is mundanely acquired. Good leaders are not one-dimensional specialists. Good leaders are the leaders with the broad-spectrum skills that enable them to meet every leadership challenge that comes their way in leadership.

4. Intellectually Capable
("And Understanding Science," v. 4d)

In the postmodern era, science seems to be dictating the pace of human endeavors. And not wanting to be left behind, disciplines in the arts have also raised the bar in an attempt to keep pace with the unassailable strides of science.

Science was also the desire of the academics, policymakers, and even kings back in Daniel's era. The centrality of science in human endeavor should be viewed against the backdrop that it holds the key, and is also the trump card to human development.

And as theology is reputed to be the father and mother of the arts and sciences, and ministry a bedmate of theology, they should function and deliver within the ambience of scientific benchmark.

To this end is the leader expected to be intellectually capable of knowing and understanding the scientific principles of leadership, versatile in the perspective of leadership, and adaptive in the face of challenges.

There is one existential truth in leadership that has stood the test of time: an ill-equipped leader produces ill-equipped results. From another angle, right input produces right output. This theory does not change anywhere, not even in hell.

5. Confidence
("As Had Ability in Them," v. 4e)

Confidence is not a gift; confidence is a skill. And as all skills are acquired and demand development, so does confidence. The attainment of confidence is not accomplished overnight. It comes through diligence and a reasonable spell of time.

The good leader is the one who is qualified in his or her field, having acquired the requisite knowledge of qualification, which invariably comes with confidence. The good and competent leader is clothed with confidence; confidence becomes the approval of such a leader.

Jesus Christ, an example in ministry, was such an incredibly confident figure that the connoisseurs were dazzled by the manner of His confidence in delivery:

> Then came the officers to the chief priests and Pharisees; and they said unto them, Why have ye not brought him? The officers answered, Never man spake like this man.
>
> —John 7:45–46

When you are confident, your speech depicts that you are. When you are confident, your walking depicts that you are. When you are confident, your gestures depict that you are. Everything about you portrays a confident person. It does not take a wish or dream to be confident; it takes only work.

6. Diplomatically Capable
("To Stand in the King's Palace," v. 4f)

One can only be with the elite if he is as cultured and refined as the elite. And one can only stand before the king after she has been thoroughly prepared for such office. All the people God chose to perform exploits on His behalf went through methodological preparations.

Consider Moses: he went through forty years of training in governance and diplomacy at the palace of Pharaoh. When he graduated, God took him into the wilderness to go through another forty years of training—this time in the school of intercession and spiritual leadership—before his commissioning in the presence of the "burning bush" (the Holy Spirit) in the wilderness:

> And the angel of the LORD appeared unto him in a flame of fire out of the midst of a bush: and he looked, and, behold, the bush burned with fire, and the bush was not consumed. And Moses said, I will now turn aside, and see this great sight, why the bush is not burnt. And when the LORD saw that he turned aside to see, God called unto him out of the midst of the bush, and said, Moses, Moses. And he said, Here am I.
>
> —Exodus 3:2-4

In ministry we can only stand before God if we are holy and pure, and can stand before the public only if we are adequately trained in our chosen profession to match or even overtake the intellectual standard of the hour.

7. Re-Orientation and Identification
("Teach the Learning and the Tongue of the Chaldeans," v. 4f)

Orientation, re-orientation and identification are major prerequisites of ministry or Christian leadership, and the significant attachment to this theme is that this process is a daily one. The leader does not merely go through a one-shot orientation and identification and receive graduation.

The stark reality in leadership principles is that one does not ever graduate the "course" of orientation and identification. It is an unending process in Christian leadership until death. Paul presents this bitter truth thus:

I am crucified with Christ: nevertheless I live; yet not I, but Christ liveth in me: and the life which I now live in the flesh, I live by the faith of the Son of God, who loved me, and gave himself for me.

—GALATIANS 2:20

8. Relativity to the Attributes of the Connected Deity ("Appointed Them a Daily Provision of the King's Meat," v. 5a)

The leader—and to a larger extent, the Christian—can only relate to God if he or she has the nature and attributes of God. This can only come through the spiritual menu we are fed.

The leader can only relate to God through the divine menu that comes from diligent study of the Word of God and the power of prayer. The Christian leader, through Word study and prayer, goes through a regimen of transformation that makes him a little bit more like God. The leader cannot transform himself of his own strength; it takes divine impartation to bring about this transformation of his nature.

9. Compatibility ("They Might Stand Before the King," v. 5b)

You cannot stand before a king if you are not compatible to his nature and what he represents.

For instance you cannot speak as a representative of the president of the United States if you are from a foreign country and of a different cultural disposition, wearing foreign clothing, only able to speak your foreign language. You would create a command barrier in this instant.

From the spiritual perspective, you cannot be lost in ungodliness and impurity and be placed before the presence of God as His representative.

Though by the theological truth, God calls the unqualified to qualify, the ministry truth is the opposite—He qualifies you before you can stand before Him. In salvation, His grace brings the sinner before God, but in ministry His Word and other impartations transform and empower us before He commissions us to stand before Him in ministry. Remember, true ministry is standing before Him to be sent to and fro.

10. Identification
("Prince of the Eunuchs Gave Names," v. 7a)

The disciples were the first to be called "Christians." They were called Christians not because they hired a marketing mogul or a versatile communication expert to market the name of Christ alongside them; their identification with Christ did that.

True Christianity is identification with Christ. Any Christian leader who has painstakingly gone through the high profile leadership prerequisites is a facsimile of God in human form on Earth.

Christianity is sick today because of the weak conviction Christians have of their salvation. And once the church is filled with parishioners whose conviction of salvation is nothing to write home about, the element of connectivity that should have existed between the church and God is so porous that divinity is no longer seen in the charactereological traits of the saints.

With the saltiness in the Christian gone, a speck of Christ can never be seen in the church, and as such Acts 11:26b shall forever remain in the archives of Christianity:

> And the disciples were called Christians first in Antioch.

11. Decisively Decisive
("Purposed in His Heart," v. 8a)

Knowledge and competence breed confidence, and confidence breeds decisiveness. All things being equal, a person of knowledge could turn out to be a competent person. A competent person with prior knowledge of his terrain is confident in policy formulation as well as in policy implementation.

There is an element of commonality among qualified, competent, and confident people: decisiveness. When you know who you are, what you have, and where you are going, you are decisive in pursuit.

Barack Obama, the current president of the United States, could do well as a president, and go into the annals of history as one of the very finest presidents America has ever had. The man is an embodiment of knowledge, competence, confidence and decisiveness. This is the source of his popularity. And the admirable feature about his decisiveness is that this virtue was mostly directed towards economic appreciation and human betterment, with militaristic decisiveness falling far below that of diplomatic decisiveness.

Christian leadership requires the decision to put "the cross before me and the world behind me."

> Looking unto Jesus the author and finisher of our faith; who for the joy that is set before him endured the cross, despising the shame, and is set down at the right hand of the throne of God.
>
> —Hebrews 12:2

12. Ensure Untainted
(That He Would Not Defile Himself With The Portion Of The King's Meat," v. 8b)

The devil dominates the carnal man through the five senses, while the sixth sense, faith, dominates the Christian, the redeemed man. This is the border between the godly and the ungodly. The sixth sense, which operates by the Word of God, censors all information received from the five senses, rejecting that which is not in conformity to the Word of God but embracing and working with that which toes the line of Scripture for the good of the recipient.

Daniel, in deciding to operate outside the five senses of seeing, hearing, feeling, tasting, and smelling, dealt a major blow to the contamination process instituted by the king, albeit indirectly through the menu served to him. Daniel's rise to fame in Babylon unveiled several principles for success. Chief among them is that great achievements do not come by chance, nor are they coincidences. If this were so, the insane man on the street of a Third World country could wake up one day to find himself sitting in the White House as the President of the United States of America.

And in studying the Messianic ministry, and the principles behind Christ's accomplishment on the cross, the character of the Messiah offers the best reference tool. Without character there can be no charisma. I am talking about pure chaste charisma, not charisma with satanic power behind it. Unfortunately, there are many satanically empowered individuals in the ministry today.

The minister of God today must not expect to be a man of the postmodern world, complying with its habits and rules, and at the same time expect to replicate the ministerial success of Daniel. Daniel was Daniel because of what he chose to eat—that is, because he chose to obey God rather than a sinful social order—and Daniel made this choice because of the nature of his character.

In ministry, we must be cautious not to fall into the trap of being swayed by the crowd or our associates. In Daniel's challenging moment, there were many Hebrew young men among his group who opted to comply with Nebuchadnezzar's rules and regulations. These went wining and dining in the order of the day while Daniel went vegetarian in pursuit of his divine identity.

The Christian leader's greatest weapons for both offense and defense are holiness and purity. Once these essential attributes are lacking in the life of the Christian leader, ministry becomes merely a profession and not a calling; and in this profession, the homosexual, the drunkard, the womanizer, the impure, and other lost sinners can all mount the podium and dish out sermonettes of intellectual excellence devoid of the seed of God, which is the only means of transforming words spoken from the podium into life for those sitting in the pew.

Conclusion

Humanity, through ministry, is privileged to cooperate with God, collaborate with God, and co-work with God—for God, in God, and to God.

With God, from the theological view that we are co-workers with God. (See 2 Corinthians 6:1.) For God, from the perspective that all that we do in the ministry is for the benefit of the kingdom of heaven. In God, in that without being imbedded in Him we are no match for Satan. And to God, based on the biblical fact that to Him is all glory ascribed, be it in ministry, business, or any other area of our lives.

Through ministry we are graciously enabled to experience in a practical way the acts from the heart of God, the thoughts of God for us through the Trinity's mind, and the power of God to us through His mind, via theology.

Through the written Word theology emerges, through theology ministry emerges, and through ministry the fivefold ministers emerge to become vessels, as it were, through whom Divinity's profound love and amazing grace are made known to fallen humanity, and shared among the brethren.

Ministry thus becomes the vehicle through which Divinity's greatest privilege, collaboration with humanity, is received and appreciated. Indeed, we mortal humans should be forever grateful to God that through ministry we are graciously allowed to share in the work of the Immortal One.

To put it mildly, God's grace is unequaled privilege, and every unequaled privilege ought to be handled without abuses, or with minimal abuse. Thus we are enjoined as the privileged co-workers of God to conduct ministry responsibly. Responsible conduct is merely a negligible token, the least we can do to show our appreciation.

Glossary

1. Differences of Administration (1 Cor. 12:5)

The Holy Spirit, the overlord and administrator of the church, has structured the gifts in a manner reflecting His ordered and specialized perspective.

The differences of administration here are akin to different branches of specialization within the medical profession. In this wise, two people could both have the gift of healing but with power over different illnesses.

For example:

1. Healing solely for the physical body
2. Healing solely for insanity

2. Diversities of Operation

1. This refers to the different levels of giftings.
2. This has to do with the manner of effecting healing through a received gift.

For example, one person could pray for a sick person and there would be healing. But another person could just clap her hands before the sick person and the same healing would result.

3. When He Ascended Up on High, He Led Captivity Captive (Eph. 4:8)

When Jesus ascended on high and was coronated by the Father God as the Lord of Lords, the first thing our Lord Jesus did was neutralize the one who had the power of captivity—Satan. The reasons for this urgent act of Jesus are as follows:

1. To break the satanic hegemony over humanity once and for all.
2. To remove any power that might stand in the way of the structures and institutions of the church (i.e., the fivefold ministers and ministries) before releasing the ministry gifts to the fivefold ministries.
3. To let Satan know that after Calvary the ultimate authority over humanity rests in the Trinity.

4. The Spirits of the Prophets Are Subject to the Prophets (1 Cor. 14:32)

The operations of the charismatic gifts, including the gift of prophecy, are subject to the control of the recipients of these gifts. In this verse, Paul zeroes in on prophecy and tongues and cautions that uncontrollable emotional ecstasy negates the authenticity of these gifts, and that their recipients must have the spiritual, mental, and physical capacity to control their operations. The Holy Spirit as the God of order does not superintend over charismatic impropriety.

5. From the Days of John the Baptist, the Kingdom of Heaven Suffereth Violence (Matt. 12:11)

John the Baptist came to unveil the ministry of our Lord Jesus Christ. The highest point in the Messianic ministry was Calvary. Jesus' death reconciled fallen man to his estranged Father, God.

At Calvary, the veil of the temple was rent, making God the Father accessible to those who, through the Messianic intermediary, seek Him. Thus from Calvary to the present, the kingdom of heaven (representing all that God stands for) can be accessed through principles anchored in faith and obedience without any intermediary priesthood.

Index of Scripture

Genesis
1:26 *6, 45*
2:2 *31, 119*
2:7 *12-13*
2:15 *47, 137*
2:16–17 *150*
2:18 *12*
11:4 *112*

Exodus
3:2 *171*
3:2–4 *171*
3:3–4 *39*
3:4 *17, 22*
3:10 *8*
4:1–4 *131*
4:16 *144*
18:16–23 *122-125*
19:18 *84*
24:15 *169*
28:41 *27*
40:35 *13*

Leviticus
1:5 *145*
4:8–10 *31*
21:10 *145*

Numbers
12:9–10 *130*

Deuteronomy
32:48–50 *153*

Joshua
1:1–2 *120*
1:2 *120*
1:10–11 *118*

Judges
13:5 *129*
13:25 *129*
16:21 *33, 134, 169*
16:30 *118*

1 Samuel
1:11 *40, 71*
3:3 *39-40*
3:19 *76*
8:4–5 *71*
9:18–19 *77*
10:1 *128, 130*
13:13 *40*
15:22 *20, 30*
16:13 *28, 73, 130, 165*

1 Kings
18:38–39 *87*

2 Kings
2:5 *75*
5:25–27 *25*
5:27 *25*

2 Chronicles
7:17–18 *41*

Psalms
8:3 *11*
8:4–5 *45*
16:8 *55*

Proverbs
4:7 *29, 157*
29:18 *149*

Isaiah
9:6 *96*
59:19 *119*

Jeremiah
1:5 *71*

Ezekiel
3:9 *7*

Daniel
11:32 *85*
12:4 *150*

Joel
2:28 *148-149*

Matthew
4:5–6 *34*
5:20 *101*
10:2 *63*
11:12 *72*
12:42 *116*

22:37 *110*
28:18–19 *21*
28:19 *80*

Mark
4:41 *110, 128*
7:37 *84, 115*
16:17 *84*
16:20 *1, 8*

Luke
4:5–6 *158*
4:6 *46*
8:28 *33*
19:10 *58*
19:13 *48*
22:41–42 *154*

John
1:11–12 *38*
5:17 *4*
7:45 *56, 102, 170*
7:45–46 *56, 102, 170*
8:12 *150*
10:11 *90*
14:1–2 *50*
14:15 *110*
20:16 *98*

Acts
2:2–4 *164*
2:3–4 *37*
2:4 *26*
2:6–9 *112*
2:7–8 *26*
2:37 *109*
5:3,5 *69*
5:5 *25*
5:12 *86*
6:3,5 *132*
6:4 *3*
6:8 *85, 133*
9:15 *136*
9:18,20 *143*
11:19 *64*
11:26 *173*
16:16–18 *77*
21:4 *67*
21:10–11 *111*
26:19–20 *30*

Romans
1:1 *20, 63*
3:23–24 *108*
6:1 *102*
8:10 *2*
10:14 *7*
11:25 *38*

1 Corinthians
1:1 *134*
2:16 *52*
3:9 *9, 78*
9:27 *34, 152*
12:4–6 *129*
12:7–11 *15*
12:8 *104, 106*
12:10 *26, 74, 78, 111*
12:11 *104*
14:3 *112*
14:29 *68, 100*
14:31 *74*

2 Corinthians
1:22 *169*
5:17 *37*
5:19 *53*
12:14 *96*

Galatians
2:20 *20, 57, 172*
5:22–23 *105*
6:10 *93*

Ephesians
2:20 *62, 69, 74, 139*
4:7 *139*
4:8–11 *59, 104*
4:11 *12, 59, 74, 78, 104, 111, 138*
4:12 *142*

Philippians
3:8 *20*
3:10 *87*
3:12 *127*
4:1 *82*

1 Timothy
1:12–13 *133*
3:6–7 *63*

2 Timothy
2:15 *98*
3:16–17 *55*
4:6–7 *64*
4:7–8 *61*

Hebrews
1:1 *7, 25, 68*
1:1–2 *7, 25, 68*
12:1 *54, 154*
12:1–2 *154*
12:2 *31, 119*
12:14 *169*
13:8 *88*

James
1:17 *151*
2:17 *116*

1 Peter
2:9 *37*

1 John
4:4 *160*

Jude
1:3 *65*

INDEX OF SUBJECTS

A

Abrahamic 39
Adam 6, 9, 11-14, 38, 44-49, 51, 56, 94, 137, 138, 150, 158
Additionally 7
Aesthetic 9
Akin 3, 5, 69, 71, 116, 128, 161, 177
Analogize 44
Anatomy 15, 17, 140, 141
Anointing 9-10, 21, 25, 2-30, 32, 37, 42, 48-49, 70, 73, 81, 87, 110, 128-130, 144-145, 164, 165, 166
Appraisal 1, 9, 17, 46, 102
Attributes 2, 6, 9, 14-15, 24, 32, 36, 44, 46, 49, 108, 137, 168, 172, 175

B

Benchmark 6, 8-9, 34, 63, 81, 105, 110, 156, 170
Bivocational 95, 96
Body 2, 11-12, 14, 15, 24-26, 28, 30-32, 34, 59, 97-99, 104-107, 109, 111-113, 119, 120, 122, 138, 141, 142, 152, 166, 177

C

Charismata 24
Chemistry 23
Church 1, 2, 3, 11-15, 17, 21, 24-27, 35, 39, 49-52, 55, 58-63, 65-69, 71, 74-77, 82, 84-89, 91, 92, 93-95, 97-100, 104-107, 111-115, 118, 121, 138, 139, 140-147, 164, 173, 177
Clarion 22, 135
Collaborator, ministry of 6
Commonality 106, 157, 173
Conflict 94-95
Congregation 13, 68, 74, 81, 85, 89, 90-91, 145
Connoisseurs 87, 170
Contemporary 9, 44-45, 47, 49, 51, 63, 64, 90, 101-103, 107, 114
Coterie 39, 67
Counseling 90-93, 96, 124, 152
Covenant 33, 39-40, 70-71
Covenantal 33, 40, 71, 134
Creation 1, 2, 5, 6, 11, 18, 31, 44, 46-47, 49-50, 52, 57, 94, 112, 115, 119, 123, 134, 137, 140, 151, 158, 163

D

Definable 1, 32
Discourse 5
Dynamic 1, 9, 100, 102, 129, 157, 160-161, 167
Dynamics 3, 94-95, 98, 102, 158, 160

E

Ear 7, 24, 81
Eden 5, 6, 9, 14, 38, 44, 45, 47-49, 91, 107, 137
Edenic 9, 12
Elastic 1, 118, 163
Employer 5
Empowered 6, 47, 63-64, 67, 134, 139, 174
Ennobled 1, 39
Evangelist 4, 39, 80-88, 103, 115, 141
Evolution 4, 11, 44, 101, 138

Experientially 49, 55, 108, 109
Exquisiteness 83-84, 115
Extendible 1
eye of, Prophetic 6
Eye, theology of 6

F

Facilitator, ministry of 6
Feasible 5, 29, 37, 56
Functionality 45, 63, 143

G

Garden 5, 6, 9, 14, 38, 44-45-48, 49, 91, 107, 137, 150
Generations 5, 18, 148, 157
Gifts 8 15-16, 19, 22, 24-27, 29, 34, 37, 39, 41, 48-49, 59, 62, 67, 72-73, 77, 80, 89, 93, 97, 99, 100, 104-113, 119, 129, 177-178
Governed 3, 49, 89, 141
Greek 5, 24, 37, 60
Guidance 5, 29, 31, 59

H

Habiru 13, 153
Heart 5, 24, 37, 46-47, 50, 69, 77, 88, 93, 94, 100, 108-110, 117, 121, 136, 173, 176
History 8, 12, 21, 28, 35, 50, 57, 71, 75, 80, 114, 133, 138, 144, 153, 164, 173
Holistic 2, 17, 37, 56, 60, 70, 81, 97, 101-102, 124, 127, 137
Homiletical, 83
Hypothesis 52, 73, 114, 137, 148

I

Immortal 47, 176
Impact 2, 18, 33, 36, 44, 53, 57, 61, 64, 70, 72, 114-115, 117, 119, 121, 123, 125, 137, 139, 141, 143, 145, 147, 149
Inconsequential 20
Indubitable 37, 54
Inferentially 37, 56, 67, 70, 72, 158
Infinitesimal 21
Influence 2, 17, 28-29, 49, 50, 56, 62, 101, 107, 114-115, 117, 119, 121, 123, 125, 130, 137, 162, 163, 164
Ingrained 160
Inherent 68, 78, 84, 129, 158, 160-161
Initiation 23, 27, 36-37, 39, 41, 43, 73, 131
Insatiable 17, 53, 81, 149
Intrusion 77, 92, 122

K

Kaleo 37
Kingdom 1, 29, 40, 41, 45, 47, 72, 80, 101, 158, 176, 178
Kinsmen 17
Knowledge 15, 16, 18, 19, 20, 25, 29, 30, 47-49, 52, 56, 61, 63-64, 75, 76, 83, 91, 105-106, 149-150, 168-170, 173

L

Latitude 1, 47
Lawyers 98
Leadership 26, 29, 51, 63, 69, 73, 89, 91, 95, 104, 122, 123-139, 141, 143, 144-145, 147, 154, 156-171, 173, 175
Levitical 27

Logos 5, 37, 52, 67, 88

M

Maid 5
Man 5-6, 11-15, 17, 21, 26, 29, 36, 37, 40, 41, 45, 47, 50, 52-53, 55-58, 63, 71-72, 75, 80, 83, 85, 87, 91, 94, 100-104, 108, 110-114, 120, 128, 132, 133, 135, 137, 150-152, 164, 166, 169, 170, 173-174, 178
Messianic 3, 55, 70, 80, 84, 115, 174, 178
Metamorphic 77
Mission 5, 8, 62, 64, 143, 145, 164
Mistress, 5
Mosaic 8, 42, 101, 122, 135, 144
Moses 8, 13-14, 17-18, 22, 23, 27-28, 38-43, 73, 84, 120, 122-124, 130-131, 134-136, 144, 153, 156-158, 160, 169, 171

N

Natural, attributes of 2
Nature 1-3, 8, 11-15, 21, 24, 29, 31, 34, 37, 44-45, 64, 74, 90, 94, 126, 138, 160, 167, 172, 174

O

Orchestra
  (see Orchestration)
Orchestration 21
Order 1, 8-9, 11, 17, 22-23, 25, 32, 36, 40-41, 45-46, 49, 50-53, 57, 66, 69, 70, 72-73, 76-78, 88, 98, 100, 105, 109-110, 115, 119, 138, 140-141, 144-145, 151, 156, 174, 178
Orderliness 49, 83, 115
Organization 15, 63, 83, 99, 114-119, 121-125, 129, 142, 143
Output 50, 70, 117, 124, 144, 152, 170
Overarching 50, 114, 137, 139, 142, 149

P

Parallelism 12
Parish 81
Pastoral 4, 80, 90, 92, 94-95, 96, 141
Pentecost 2, 3, 60, 84, 112, 139, 164
Periodic 1, 9, 66, 87

Permeate 14
Perspective 5-6, 11-12, 14, 17, 28, 32, 49, 52, 56, 61, 63, 67, 72, 74, 77, 80, 91, 94, 102, 110, 119, 120, 126, 132, 134, 137, 144, 149, 156, 161, 163, 167, 170, 172, 176-177
Pervade 22
Pervasive 1, 36, 44, 90, 123, 129, 153, 162, 169
Pew 86, 175
Physical 2-3, 22, 29-32, 63, 65, 80, 91, 127, 130, 143, 177-178
Pinnacle 2, 24, 33, 47
Pivotal 80
Postulation 115
Prayer 3, 21, 27, 35, 69, 72-73, 77, 85-86, 106, 172
Preamble 21, 25
Principles 3, 24, 48, 56, 60, 102, 122, 129-130, 142, 156-157, 160-162, 165, 168, 170-171, 174, 178
Prophet 4, 39, 62, 67-79, 81-82, 87, 103, 111, 130, 139, 141
Prophetic, eye of 6
Pseudo 77
Purification 23

Q

Qualities 18, 76, 83, 85, 100, 117, 123, 126, 132-133, 135, 143, 158, 168
Queen 5, 116
Quintessence, 52, 69, 71, 102, 121, 164

R

Rabbi 98
Rabboni 98
Ramah 28, 71, 73, 131, 165
Responsiveness 22, 23

S

Sacred, 27, 34
Samuelic 18
Scrutiny 45, 71, 99
Senses 6, 42-43, 54, 154, 166, 174
Shepherd 82, 89-90, 92, 96
Skepticism 22
Skills 9, 49, 132, 161, 169, 170
Solitary 11, 17, 29, 123, 154
Spectrum 36, 67, 169
Stages 11, 19, 151

Structure 12-13, 45, 62, 66, 76, 114, 121, 123, 125, 137-140, 145, 147, 162
Subjection 34, 152
Sublime 17, 39, 45, 104, 151
Succinctly 41
Surplus 80
Sustenance 5, 37, 102, 165

T

Technology 9, 51
Theology 1, 4-9, 11, 21, 30, 38, 76, 91, 137-138, 156, 170, 176
Theos 5
Tools 24, 47
Tripartite 45
Trouble
  (see Troubleshooters) 2
Typology 5

U

Unambiguously 78
Unchangeability 44
Underlying 48, 56, 75, 113
Unrivaled 80, 144

V

Venturing 21
Virtues 9, 15, 19, 24, 33, 44, 57, 73, 78, 84, 107, 109, 133-34

W

Walks 6, 116
Wanton 24
Weeping 87-88
Whisked 28, 75
Wisdom 15, 16, 25, 29, 48-49, 69, 75, 76, 81, 84-85, 97, 105-106, 116, 118, 132-133, 156-157, 164, 169
Word 3, 5, 8, 13, 15-16, 18, 25-26, 29, 30, 32-33, 37, 45, 48, 52-57, 60-61, 63-64, 67-70, 72, 74-78, 82,-86, 88-89, 98-99, 102, 105, 106, 109-111, 137, 140, 142-143, 148, 150, 159, 164, 172, 174, 176
Workers 18, 21, 144, 176

Y

Yahweh 46, 165, 169

BIBLIOGRAPHY

Aldrich, Joseph C. *Life-Style Evangelism*. Portland: Multnomah Press,1978.

Alsop, Bill. *Mantled with Power*. Raleigh, NC: Anointed to Serve Ministries, 1997.

Bryant, T. A. *Today's Dictionary of the Bible*, Minneapolis: Bethany House Publishers, 1982.

Burns, Robert A. *Roman Catholicism*. Chicago: Loyola University Press, 1992.

Henry, Carl F. H. *God, Revelation and Authority*. Waco, TX: Word Books Publisher, 1966.

Carter, John D. *The Integration of Psychology and Theology*. Grand Rapids, MI: Zondervan Publishing House, 1979.

Dyrness, William. *Themes in Old Testament Theology*. Downers Grove, IL: InterVarsity Press, 1971.

Eichrodt, Walter. *Theology of the Old Testament*. Philadelphia: Westminster Press, 1967.

Geisler, Norman L. *Christian Apologetics*. Grand Rapids, MI: Baker Book House, 1976.

Getz, Gene. *Loving One Another*. Downers Grove, IL: InterVarsity Press, 1984.

Groothuis, Douglas. *Confronting the New Age*. Downers Grove, IL: InterVarsity Press, 1988.

Hagin, Kenneth E. *The Triumphant Church*. Tulsa: Faith Library Press, 2006.

Hammond, Frank D. *Overcoming Rejection*. Kirkwood, MO: Impact Christian Books, 1987.

Harris, Hall W. III. *The Descent of Christ*. Grand Rapids, MI: Baker Book House, 1996.

Lockyer, Herbert. *All the Prayers of the Bible*. Grand Rapids, MI: Zondervan Publishing House, 1959.

———. *All the Christians of the Bible*. Grand Rapids, MI: Zondervan Publishing House, 1970.

Logan, Kevin. *Satanism and the Occult*. Eastbourne: Kingsway Publication, 1994.

Martin, Walter. *The Kingdom of the Cults*. Minneapolis: Bethany Book House, 1985.

Moody, D. L. *Secret Power*. New Kensington, PA: Whitaker House, 1997.

Padovani, Martin H. *Healing Wounded Emotions*. Michigan: Twenty-Third Publications, 1987.

Parker, J.L. *God Has Spoken*. Downers Grove, IL: InterVarsity Press, 1979.

Pentecost, Dwight J. *Things to Come*. Grand Rapids, MI: Zondervan Publishing House, 1964.

Pink, Arthur W. *The Antichrist*. Grand Rapids, Michigan: Kregel Publications, 1988.

Robertson, A. T. *A Harmony of the Gospel*. New York: Harper and Row, 1990.

Rogers, Harold *The One You Can Become*. Nashville, TN: Abingdon, 1978.

Ryrie, Charles. *Basic Theology*. Chicago: Moody Press, 1999.

Schemer, Kenneth E. *Between Faith and Tears*. Nashville, TN: Thomas Nelson Publishers, 1981.

Silva, Moises. *Biblical Words and Their Meaning*. Grand Rapids, MI: Zondervan Publishing House, 1994.

Shryock, Harold. You and Your Health. Lincolnshire: Strasborough Press, 1998.

Sproul, P. C. *The Last Days According to Jesus*. Grand Rapids, MI: Baker Book House, 1998.

Virkler, Henry A. *Hermeneutics*. Grand Rapids, MI: Baker Book House, 1992.

Walton, Rus. *One Nation Under God*. Old Tappan, NJ: Fleming H. Revell Company, 1975.

Warren, Rick. *The Purpose Driven Life*. Grand Rapids, MI: Zondervan Publishing House, 2002.

Other Books by the Author

Total Prayer

Biblical Principles of Appreciation

21st Century Leadership

NOTES

Chapter 6

1. Walter Eichrodt, *Theology of the Old Testament* (Philadelphia: Westminster Press, 1967), 31.
2. Rick Warren, *The Purpose Driven Church* (Grand Rapids, MI: Zondervan, 1995), 374.

Chapter 7

1. Eichrodt, 16.
2. Eichrodt, 24.
3. Norman L. Geisler, *Christian Apologetics* (Grand Rapids, MI: Baker Book House, 1976), 77.
4. Warren, 332.
5. Ibid., 38.
6. Ibid., 301.
7. Ibid., 253.
8. Ibid., 334.
9. Dwight J. Pentecost, *Things to Come* (Grand Rapids, MI: Zondervan, 1964), 580.

Chapter 9

1. Warren, 86.

Chapter 10

1. Bill Alsop, *Mantled with Power* (Raleigh, NC: Anointed to Serve Ministries, 1997), 12.

Chapter 12

1. Warren, 295.
2. Alvin S. Undgren, *Foundations for Purposeful Church Administration* (Nashville, TN: Adingen Press, 1988), 121.

Chapter 14

1. Alsop, 1.
2. Smith Wigglesworth, *Power to Serve* (New Kensington, PA: Whitaker House, 1998), 9.

Chapter 15

1. Rick Warren, *The Purpose Driven Life* (Grand Rapids, MI: Zondervan, 2002), 202.

Chapter 16

1. LeRoy Eims, *Be the Leader You Were Meant to Be* (Wheaten, IL: Victor Books, 1975), 8.

About the Author

DR. P. MYLES-AIKINS, AN eminent authority in Ministry and a gifted conference speaker with the passion for revival is the General Overseer of Amazing Grace Church International, Tema, Ghana. A graduate of CFNI, Dallas, Texas, he received his BTh, MMin, and DMin from the International Seminary, Florid, and his PhD (Th), PhD (Min, summa cum laude) from the Evangel Christian University, Louisiana.

Contact the Author

Telephone: (610) 504-0012

(301) 728-0198

E-mail: papamyles.aikins@yahoo.com

www.pmylesaikins.com

www.ingramcontent.com/pod-product-compliance
Lightning Source LLC
Chambersburg PA
CBHW062217080426
42734CB00010B/1920